Studying the Holocaust

D0238060

Studying the Holocaust provides a guide to the philosophical, historical and moral issues involved when studying or teaching the Holocaust.

There is now an increasing readiness to view the Holocaust as a crucial reference point for multi-cultural, humanistic and liberal education. This work is designed to provide a unique source of help both to students and teachers in many fields including history, education, literature and religious education. This invaluable aid includes:

- an historical overview of the Holocaust
- key archival material, with helpful introductions
- a range of readings, questions and ideas for stimulating discussion
- an examination of the nature of the crime of genocide
- a reference section containing brief biographies of key figures and a glossary of essential terms
- a useful review of the historiography of Holocaust scholarship

Ronnie S. Landau is Director of the British Holocaust Education Project and Member of Faculty at Leo Baeck College, London, where he lectures in modern Jewish history. Former Head of Humanities at the City Literary Institute, he is author of *The Nazi Holocaust* (1992).

Studying the Holocaust

Issues, Readings and Documents

Ronnie S. Landau

London and New York

First published 1998 by Routledge
11 New Fetter Lane, London EC4P 4EE

Simultaneously published in the USA and Canada
by Routledge
29 West 35th Street, New York, NY 10001

Typeset in Galliard and Gill by Keystroke, Jacaranda Lodge, Wolverhampton
Printed and bound in Great Britain by Clays Ltd, St Ives PLC

British Library Cataloguing in Publication Data
A catalogue record for this book is available from the British Library

Library of Congress Cataloging in Publication Data
A catalogue record for this book has been requested

ISBN 0–415–16143–6
ISBN 0–415–16144–4 (pbk)

For Nicki and Leora

Contents

PART II Selected key documents   49

PART III Genocide in the modern era   89

PART IV Questions, themes and reading lists   121

Maps

Source of maps: Martin Gilbert, *The Dent Atlas of the Holocaust* (Dent, 1993), Maps nos. 6, 20, 99 and 316

Preface

This present work is intended as an educational guide, for use both independently and in conjunction with other works by teachers, students, youth leaders and, indeed, by anyone engaged in the educational process, whether formal or informal. This multi-disciplinary collection comprises educational exercises, historical documents, questions intended for reflection, class discussion and written response, literary reconstructions (it will be made abundantly clear where a reading or exercise is derivative and fictitious), historical case studies of the crime of genocide in the modern age, a chronology of the Nazi period including the Holocaust years, a glossary of terms relating to the subject, brief biographical notes of the principal characters in this historical episode, and a select bibliography. It will, I hope, prove a helpful aid to those teaching or studying this challenging subject at a variety of levels and in fields as diverse as history, psychology, literature, drama, humanities, religious studies, social studies, moral philosophy and general studies.

Acknowledgements

I should like to express my deep gratitude to Dr Mark Levene of Warwick University for his assistance in my preparation of Part III 'Genocide in the Modern Era'. Numerous other scholars, educators, students, curators and librarians have also offered me their thoughts and creative suggestions. I am indebted to them all.

I gratefully acknowledge the following authors, editors, publishing houses and educational teams, from whose illuminating works excerpts have been painstakingly selected (from literally thousands of possible pieces) for inclusion in this work:

Alternatives in Religious Education, Denver, Colorado (educational materials adapted); Facing History and Ourselves National Foundation; Yitzhak Arad, Yisrael Gutman and Abraham Margaliot (eds), *Documents on the Holocaust: Selected Sources on the Destruction of the Jews of Germany and Austria, Poland and the Soviet Union* (Yad Vashem Publications, Jerusalem 1981); Elie Cohen, *Human Behaviour in the Concentration Camps* (W. Norton, 1953); Lucy Dawidowicz, *A Holocaust Reader* (Behrman House, 1976); Alexander Donat, *The Holocaust Kingdom* (Holt, Rinehart and Winston, 1965); Gustav Gilbert, *Nuremberg Diary* (Farrer, Straus & Giroux, 1974); Emil Fackenheim, foreword to Yehuda Bauer, *The Jewish Emergence from Powerlessness* (Toronto University Press, 1979); Martin Gilbert, *Atlas of the Holocaust* (Dent, 1993); Yisrael Gutman and Chaim Schatzker, *The Holocaust and its Significance* (Zalman Shazar Center, 1984); Rudolf Hoess, *Commandant of Auschwitz: The Autobiography of Rudolf Hoess* (Weidenfeld and Nicolson, 1959); Richard Kalfus, 'Euphemisms of Death: Interpreting a Primary Source Document' (unpublished, Yad Vashem collection of educational resources); Zvi Kolitz in Albert Friedlander (ed.), *Out of the Whirlwind: A Reader of Holocaust Literature* (Schocken Books, 1976); Paul Massing, *Rehearsal for Destruction: A Study of Political Antisemitism in Imperial Germany* (Harper and Row, 1949); Paul Mendes-Flohr and Jehuda Reinharz (eds), *The Jew in the Modern World* (Oxford University Press, 1980); Stanley Milgram in *TV Guide*, 21 August 1976, quoted in *The Holocaust Years: Society on Trial* (B'nai B'rith Anti-Defamation League, 1979); Jeremy Noakes and Geoffrey Pridham (eds), *Nazism 1919–1945. A*

Documentary Reader, 4 vols. (Exeter University Press, Vols I and II 1984, Vol. III 1988 and Vol. IV 1997); Maurice Ogden, 'The Hangman' (Regina Publications); Elie Wiesel, *Legends of Our Time* (Holt, Rinehart and Winston, 1968); and, especially, I.B. Tauris, London and Ivan R. Dee, Chicago, who published – in Britain and the USA respectively – my earlier work *The Nazi Holocaust*, from which some material has been both included and adapted.

Introduction
The Holocaust as educational theme

Prologue

This book addresses head-on one of the most harrowing, perplexing and – for many – incomprehensible of educational themes; a subject that is frankly difficult to reconcile with much of what we are generally prepared to associate with the human condition and the realm of human possibilities.

Yet human history can be looked at in many different ways. To take two opposing approaches, we can see it, on the one hand, as essentially a grim record of the big and the strong attempting to dominate those who are smaller and weaker. Or, on the other hand, taking a more positive view, we may see it as broadly the story of individuals and groups trying to solve problems – be they ethical, political, social or scientific.

Of all animals, only humans control both their environment and their development, and only we can be held morally accountable for our actions. The staggering speed of our technological advance contrasts depressingly with the slow, halting pace of our ethical 'progress': we may travel in space, cruise the information superhighway and watch the Olympic Games beamed by satellite – simultaneously and instantaneously – to every part of the globe; yet still we have widespread slavery, racial discrimination, starvation and injustice. (Indeed, space travel and satellite technology are themselves by-products of the nuclear arms race.) These contradictions and ambiguities are inherent in our existence on this planet and no single historical event has, I believe, the power to draw them into sharper focus than the subject of this book.

The unparalleled catastrophe that overwhelmed the Jews of Europe during the period 1941–45 can now be said to constitute not only one of the most horrendous but arguably one of the most significant events of modern world history. The Holocaust or, as it is known much more satisfyingly in Hebrew, the 'Shoah', is no longer reduced to the status of footnote to the Second World War – its 'explanation' lying merely in the barbarity to which human-kind had been reduced by the extremities of international warfare – nor is it explained away by a variety of simple, one-dimensional theories, for example 'the Holocaust was just an extreme example of human prejudice' or 'it was essentially the product of "scapegoating"' or – most crass of all – of something peculiarly 'German'. Rather it is now seen as a complex subject with its own distinctive history and internal 'logic'. Above all, it is an historical event that seems to issue the most terrifying warnings to us all about the darker side of our own nature and of the societies we have created and, in particular, the dangers inherent in our modern political systems, our technological inventiveness and our bureaucratic processes.

The Holocaust has, in effect, become a central reference point for humanity as we look forwards with hope into the new millennium, while at the same time throwing a backwards glance – in fear, guilt and shame – at the blood-drenched century we are leaving behind; a twentieth century from which we should like, perhaps, to learn some lessons. If we are to have a future, the Holocaust seems to tell us, we must surely remember our past.

But it was not always so. For almost twenty years after the war, historians, educationalists and philosophers maintained an eerie, if reverential, silence on the subject, especially its moral and historical significance. It was the trial in 1961 of former SS bureaucrat Adolf Eichmann, one of the principal architects of the 'Final Solution' – a trial held controversially in Israel and very much a 'show' trial designed to educate the Israeli public -- that represented a watershed in our consciousness of the educational importance of this event. This was followed soon afterwards by the Cuban missile crisis, during which the world seemed to be teetering on the brink of nuclear catastrophe, and then by the assassination of US President John F. Kennedy, another epoch-marking event which struck such a chord of emotion and insecurity.

It was these events, coming so close together, that seemed to awaken a serious and hitherto – for the most part – repressed interest in the subject of the Holocaust, a trend that has grown appreciably in the ensuing decades. For since the mid-1960s, it has been the immediate present, with all its unsettled problems, that has contributed to the burgeoning interest in the Nazi onslaught: Vietnam, Biafra, various Middle East wars, Cambodia, Lebanon, unresolved economic crises, 'Third World' starvation, growing alarm about the planet's future, threatened by the twin dangers of ecological and intercontinental ballistic nuclear annihilation (the MAD weapons of Mutually Assured Destruction) and an increasing awareness throughout the 1970s and 1980s of the curse of powerlessness that afflicts so many groups and individuals in today's society. All of these concerns can be related, and have been related, to the Holocaust, which has become to some almost a frame of reference, conscious or unconscious, and at times, it must be said, a somewhat misunderstood, overused and superficial one at that.

In short, more than fifty years after the defeat of Nazi Germany, one can say with assurance that the sense of awe that surrounds the Holocaust may still be there – well, generally so – but no longer the silence.

And yet there seems no other topic so emotive, so bursting at the seams with contradictory and disturbed passions, with political and spiritual conflicts, with guilt, accusations and the perhaps inevitable descent into defensiveness, apologetics and self-obsession.

One crucial consideration, therefore, that informs my approach to the subject is this: to teach the Holocaust responsibly involves a whole series of delicate balancing acts. (See Appendix G 'Teaching the Holocaust' for a considerations/dilemmas chart originally designed for teachers as an accompaniment to training seminars.) So appalling and highly charged a subject as this has, perhaps inescapably, generated a powerful and at times extremist literature, requiring the reader to pick his or her way through a minefield of different views and often emotional perspectives.

The Holocaust has at times been hijacked by various groups, each with their own ideological, political or educational preference. It is, indeed, difficult to conceive of any subject that has been quite so regularly misunderstood, misused and misrepresented by those who may be historians, educators, politicians, philosophers and communal leaders. At times, both teacher and student will have to tread a path between polar opposite views, recognizing that both positions may contain merit but that neither conveys a wholly accurate truth.

This situation places a special responsibility on the shoulders of those charged with the task of transmitting memory of this event from generation to generation, and of conveying its impact and most compellingly relevant lessons – in their classrooms, lecture theatres, conferences and tutorials. It will often take the form of encouraging students to ask – rather than necessarily answer – the most important questions raised by this subject.

The continuing relevance of the Holocaust

The Holocaust occurred long before many of us were born, and perhaps when contemplating this event we have been tempted to pass judgement on the 'passive' behaviour of our parents' and grandparents' generations. It was, and is, of course, easy and eminently satisfying for us to adopt this morally superior stance, for it allows us to put a distance between ourselves and this gruesome historical tale. We can imagine – as if we were watching a 'western' – that gripping and fascinating though the storyline is, it has precious little to do with us. The good guys and bad guys are clearly discernible; it is surely a black-and-white story and quite, quite, remote – thank goodness – from our own lives.

Yet, within the past few years, while most of *us* sat idly by, many hundreds of thousands of civilians in the former Yugoslavia – in a *European* country where many of us booked our vacations only a few short summers ago – have had their civil, national and human rights trampled underfoot, have been forcibly displaced and, in countless cases, raped, tortured and murdered. Our governments and other agencies failed utterly to make an effective intervention until it was too late. What was essentially a savage war of national aggression and 'genocide' was dignified and softened by the term 'civil war', a curious juxtaposition of words (war is never 'civil') intended to excuse our inaction – to the everlasting shame of our political leaders and of those of us old enough to vote or write letters to our newspapers and politicians.

That an international war crimes tribunal has been established to investigate and bring to justice those held responsible for 'war crimes' and 'crimes against humanity' in the former Yugoslavia is certainly a welcome development. It may even prove to have far-reaching implications for the future, especially the future safety, of minority groups. But if it is to do more than merely make *us* feel better – a kind of happy Hollywood ending to the grimmest of stories – and have the desired preventive and educational effect, it would be as well to examine the mistakes of the past fifty plus years, in particular the consistent unwillingness and apparent inability of the member-states of the United Nations to intervene in the 'sovereign affairs' of one of their own number, and their consequent failure to invoke the United Nations Genocide Convention of 1948. For *despite* the previous experience of the Nazi Holocaust, man-made catastrophes since the Second World War have by no means been limited to horrendous events in Bosnia.

The Holocaust as 'human' event (as a tale of humanity)

We are living out the last years of a century of unspeakable genocide. Though it has recently been fashionable to term it 'ethnic cleansing', whichever word is used it is the same crime – that of genocide – which is continuing to disfigure the planet, and it should be the duty of any teacher, and arguably student, of the Holocaust to attempt to understand why it occurs and how it can, in the future, be prevented. Serious educational courses on the Holocaust, therefore, as well as investigating the specific historical event, should aim to help students comprehend the carnage in Bosnia and Rwanda. This can and, I would argue, should be done without in any way diluting the significance, integrity and unique qualities of the Holocaust.

Nothing is less likely to facilitate such a grasp than the tendency to dehumanize Hitler, Nazism and the crime itself as evils which somehow lie beyond the range of our human perception and our understanding. Such 'demonization', as it has been called, is, of course, reminiscent of the medieval, often Christian, view of the Devil as the source of all evil – a remote and extraneous entity over which we humans exercise no control. This demonization leads to an obsession with evil as a purely external force, preventing us from searching for it inside ourselves and, most significantly, within the societies, technological systems and bureaucratic structures we have created.

The German perpetrators of the Holocaust (and their non-German accomplices) *were* human beings operating in human society and, to that extent, there must be a universal and humanly graspable explanation, however improbable and repellent, of their sentiments and of their behaviour. Such an approach would be none the worse for operating across cultural and national boundaries. If there are any lessons to be derived from the Holocaust there is no sense whatever in attributing its execution to Satanic monsters, for then it becomes irrelevant to what is humanly intelligible. What is more, such an interpretation of Nazism would involve an abstract dehumanization of Nazis – and often indiscriminately of all Germans – which was precisely the Nazi attitude towards Jews. An excellent example of how to avoid this pitfall and how to achieve something that is of genuine educational value is Gitta Sereny's recent book, *Albert Speer, His Battle With Truth* (Macmillan, 1995). This work succeeds in making the Nazi leadership come alive as human beings, inviting not sympathy and identity (as one critic wrote) but a rare glimpse into, and the beginning of an understanding of, the *human* face of 'evil'.

The attempt to describe the Holocaust and, by extension, much of the history of antisemitism as the product of something quintessentially and demonically 'German' is not only alarmingly wide of the mark in terms of its grasp of European and Jewish history but, more to the point, education-ally self-defeating. As a corollary to this, those of us who are Jewish should, when contemplating the Holocaust, resist our inclination – understandable, perhaps, in the face of the enormity of the trauma suffered – to see only 'Jewish' lessons and implications, and to enter some sort of exclusive Jewish claim to the event (and by extension to all 'real' genocide). What has some-times followed – and this is deeply regrettable and invariably has the unhelp-ful effect of alienating and, of course, exempting those outside the victim group – is a grotesque competition in suffering. ('Look!' some victims seem to say, 'Mine [my suffering, that is] is bigger than yours! Only *my* genocide is therefore real [*sic*] genocide.')

The unique and the universal

Without losing sight of the incomparable uniqueness of the Holocaust *as an entire event*, it is educationally essential and, therefore, legitimate to break it down into a range of more limited human experiences, motives, crises and responses, with which it might be easier to identify and which can even stand limited comparison with other predicaments and historical episodes. For, like all good education, understanding the Holocaust is ultimately about the making of *connections*.

By way of example, the legal assault launched by the Nazi state against the Jews of Germany during the period 1933–39, which foreshadowed and paved the way for the annihilation that followed, can be related to attempts by some other societies to marginalize and exclude whole groups by *process of law*, for instance the operation of apartheid in South Africa (which did not, as we now know, lead historically to genocide but always had the potential to do so).

The utter *senselessness* of the annihilation of Jews, provoked by the imagined threat they posed to German civilization, evokes memories of the Armenian genocide at the hands of the Turks in 1915, a tragedy that was also enacted against the camouflage of a world war. This set a horrifying precedent of genocide and world indifference that seemed to convince Hitler, for one, that the international community would always be prepared to turn the other way and consign even the worst atrocities to oblivion (see Hitler's speech to his army chiefs quoted on p.91).

The sheer *powerlessness, lack of choice* and *isolation* of the Jewish victims of Nazi terror anticipates, to some degree, the similar condition of the cowed and bemused victims of the systematic massacre of the Cambodian people in the mid-1970s.

The *self-righteousness* of many of the Nazi perpetrators – the prevalent belief in the correctness and 'holiness' of their bloodthirsty undertaking – can be related to almost every massacre in human history that has been carried out in the name of a religious or imperial mission, for example the murderous behaviour, over many centuries, of the Christian Spanish and their descendants in parts of South America and the racist attitude, under an anti-communist banner, of some Americans towards the Vietnamese people – both civilians and their 'legitimate' enemy – during the 1960s and 1970s.

Most critically, the *indifference* of the silent majority to the misery and suffering of others can be related to that indifference, of which most of us are guilty most of the time, to the misery and suffering of others, not merely in distant parts of the globe but also in our own countries, towns, neighbourhoods and schools.

And, finally, staying within the Nazi period itself, while Nazi attitudes and intentions towards literally millions of representatives of other victim groups – Gypsies, socialists, homosexuals, Jehovah's Witnesses, prisoners of war, Slavs – were, without question, rather different from their manic, no-exceptions view of their 'Satanic' Jewish 'enemy', if we were merely to compare the level of *individual suffering*, it would be difficult to sustain the argument that there was a real difference.

These partial analogies are not, of course, exact but they may be explored; superficial comparisons are undesirable but so is the refusal to allow any comparison. To compare two events does not imply that one causes the other; it does not assert that they are identical; it does not deny unique components.

If, on the other hand, the Holocaust is cordoned off entirely from all other subjects, from the rest of human experience and even from other people's experiences during the Second World War, it will become inaccessible – an impossibly grim and remote area of study enacted in an educationally meaningless vacuum.

Unlike those historians who make a case for the exclusiveness and uniqueness of the Holocaust only by playing down the suffering of other groups throughout history – Steven Katz is perhaps the most extreme of such historians (see select bibligraphy on p.129) – educators might wish to approach the lessons of the subject in more universal, humanistic terms. We should start – and for some this is a painful process – to see the Holocaust as more than a symbol of Jewish fate, Jewish unity and the need for Jewish survival. It is all of these but it is also a major challenge to assumptions about 'progress' and 'civilization'. The Holocaust shattered Europe-centred, liberal dreams of western reason and culture as forces that necessarily sensitize and humanize us and which promote genuine tolerance of difference. It also destroyed, once and for all, the tottering belief that science and technology were securely harnessed for the good of humanity, as scientists, politicians, bureaucrats and generals found the means progressively to give destructive expression to their beliefs and fantasies.

Shortly after the First World War, Albert Einstein, alarmed by human-kind's misuse of science, had written:

> In the hands of our generation these hard-won instruments are like a razor wielded by a child of three. The possession of marvellous means of production has brought misery and hunger instead of freedom.

In this regard it is worth reflecting for a moment on the whole history of how human beings have dealt death to one another: the progressive 'bureau-cratization' of killing has placed a steadily increasing distance between the perpetrators and the consequences of their decisions and actions.

As several educationalists and philosophers have pointed out, the Holo-caust can also be interpreted as a metaphor for the darker side of modernity. It was, in part, the outcome of problems of identity – the alienation and isolation of the individual in our modern mass societies, which have become so depersonalized and conformist. Nazism appealed to people's need for a sense of belonging, loyalty and community left dangerously unfulfilled by modern, vast, centralized society. It encouraged a psychological state whereby people could easily be sucked into the entire bureaucratic process. Bureaucracy is a human invention that can subjugate its inventor, undermine human conscience and allow individuals to abdicate personal moral responsibility. 'It's the system's fault, not mine!'

The Holocaust also raises profound and disturbing questions about the ease with which people can fall into a pattern of conformity and obedience to orders, particularly if those orders emanate from a source that is deemed to possess 'authority'.

> When you look at the long and gloomy history of man you will find more hideous crimes have been committed in the name of obedience than have ever been committed in the name of rebellion.
>
> (C. P. Snow)

The unique and important lessons of the Holocaust should not be sought in the specific and horrific details of its execution – sadly mass brutality and slaughter are far from new in human history – nor in the behaviour, psychology, religion or ethics of the Jews who were its victims. As has already been implied earlier in this chapter, its uniqueness has remarkably little to do with the harrowing experiences of individual victims. Instead, it lies in the *intentions* of its perpetrators and in the fact that these intentions were, for the most part, translated into reality – for the Jews were the only group marked out for total European annihilation (with the possible exception of those Gypsies defined by the Nazis as 'non-Aryan'), even in neutral countries and those not yet conquered. And this can, and must, be stated without diminishing in any way the suffering of any other group.

The uniqueness of the Holocaust also lies in the unprecedented way that the full might of a twentieth-century, industrially advanced state could be perverted, subordinated to a philosophy of destruction and then directed against a vulnerable, conspicuous, powerless and largely unresisting target.

The Holocaust was a totality – a global event. It was, to be sure, made up of the sum of countless individual stories, attitudes, reactions and dilemmas, but it is also much more than the sum of those parts and cannot be adequately perceived through the prism of any one component. The Holocaust had no precedent and, as an entire event, is a unique phenomenon that resists satisfactory explanation. It was, of course, a Jewish tragedy, but it was not only a Jewish tragedy; it also belongs to world history and to the realm of general humanities and moral studies. Jews, as the special victims of this unique event, are not the only possible victims of such man-made catastrophes, and their wretched experience has implications that go way beyond the Jewish world – implications of concern to the general historian, psychologist, theologian and educationalist.

The central role of questions

The attempt to come to terms with this historical event and to grapple, whether as student or as teacher, with its most important messages is an extremely difficult, not to say intimidating task. Despite the growth of a virtual Holocaust literary industry – at times it seems we have reached 'information overload' (allegedly producing a kind of 'Holocaust fatigue') – there is still no consensus, even on centrally important issues, among historians, psychologists, educationalists, theologians and philosophers. On many of the open-ended questions this topic throws up, no adequate or simple explanation is possible or, indeed, desirable. I would, therefore, emphasize the central need in Holocaust education for the formulation of questions rather than the provision of hard-and-fast answers. There are occasions, arguably many occasions, when we should merely try to identify the right *questions* and then work towards the possible answers and lessons to be inferred.

   This is easier said than done, particularly in a scholastic environment where clear answers are commonly expected from those entrusted with the task of education. At an early stage, the student of the Holocaust must try to rise above the need to stick explanatory labels on everything, and to resist the compulsion to reach precise, unequivocal conclusions in answer to the 'big' questions. Such key questions would include the following:

1 How, why and when did the Nazis determine a policy of total annihilation of the Jews of Europe?
2 To what extent was the ferocity of the Nazi onslaught rooted in the peculiar social, economic and psychological circumstances prevailing in Germany in the years following her traumatic defeat in the First World War and the humiliating Treaty of Versailles?
3 Can Germany's descent to barbarism be attributed, to any degree, to a fear of Bolshevism?
4 Is it true that full-blooded Nazi anti-Jewishness had only a very marginal appeal to ordinary Germans, even among those who voted for Hitler?
5 Why did a higher proportion of Jews survive in Fascist Italy and in countries allied to Germany, such as Rumania and Hungary, than in anti-Nazi Holland with its democratic tradition and long history of toleration towards Jews? Why did so many Jews die in Poland? Does the explanation lie in the religious antisemitism of the indigenous population? Or is the answer much more complex?
6 How on earth was it possible for such a supposedly 'civilized' society, which had given us Goethe, Beethoven and Brahms, to produce such barbarity, albeit of a largely dispassionate and coolly executed kind?
7 How are we to assess the role of the Reich railway officials who drew up rail schedules and even charged 'package tour' fares to unwitting passengers who were then transported in cattle trucks to extermination camps in the east?
8 How was it possible for certain individuals, whose role would prove indispensable to the carrying out of the 'Final Solution of the Jewish Question', to be subtly conditioned into believing that to kill Jews was morally no worse than to brush dandruff off their jackets – and, on the contrary, was a morally good thing?
9 Why do the Jews *appear* to have offered so little resistance everywhere? (Is that even the right question?)
10 How can we begin to evaluate the degree of moral responsibility of the Jewish leaders and the specially established Jewish police force in the ghettos of Poland?
11 How are we to judge the behaviour and responsibility of numerous other groups: ordinary Germans; the citizens of defeated and occupied countries; Germany's allies, such as Italy and Hungary; the various Churches throughout Europe; the anti-Nazi Allies, in particular Great

Britain, the USA and the Soviet Union; neutral governments, like those of Sweden, Switzerland, Spain and Eire; and, finally, the Jews themselves?

12 How big a factor is the astonishing human capacity for indifference to the plight of others (present in all societies and arguably on the increase) in explaining the path to Auschwitz and Treblinka?

13 What does the methodical slaughter of 1.5 million Jewish children say about the presence or interest of (a) God in human affairs? (This book will not even attempt to wrestle with such theological problems – it is beyond its scope – though other works which address such issues are cited in the bibliographies in Part IV.)

14 What is the relationship between Nazi anti-Jewish ideology and earlier expressions of anti-Judaism and antisemitism in European history?

15 What was the difference between the Jewish experience of Nazism and that of the 5.5 million other civilians – Gypsies, Poles, Russians, homosexuals, Jehovah's Witnesses, communists, socialists and others – who were also murdered in cold blood? In other words, why does the term 'Holocaust' strictly refer to the Jewish experience alone?

16 And, finally, a question that dominates Holocaust literature: is this catastrophe that overwhelmed the Jews of Europe an incomparably unique historical phenomenon, or is it a case within the category of 'genocide'?

Our emotional and intellectual helplessness in the face of the enormity of the Holocaust has led many of the 'victim group' – understandably perhaps – to seek to monopolize the event and to be disinclined to 'share' it with others. This tendency has expressed itself, at times, as a stubborn insistence that the Holocaust cannot be related to other human events and historical occurrences.

On the contrary, we must understand that the Holocaust, for all its freakishness, *was* a human event – all too human – which shows that humanity is eminently capable of doing anything that our technology makes possible, horrifyingly ready to perform unimagined acts of wholesale destruction and self-destruction. The Holocaust, to paraphrase Samuel Pisar, a survivor of Auschwitz, was not, as he thought at the time, the end of the world, but possibly, if we ignore its universal implications, the *beginning* of the end of the world.

Humankind is also, the Holocaust shows us, alarmingly prone, especially in the twentieth century, to replacing personal ethical standards with collective ones that appear to exempt the individual from accountability. However, the Holocaust gives evidence that the best is also in us, for some, in their exercise of moral choice, chose good against the polluted stream.

Educational conception and approach

Under the auspices of the British Holocaust Education Project, I consulted and interviewed many teachers and lecturers to gauge their views, experiences and preferences. This work and its underlying educational principles are to some extent, therefore, a response to a whole range of different professional opinions and perspectives on this subject. What emerged with almost audible insistence from the educators interviewed was the desire for a balanced approach that avoided, as far as possible, the extreme, subjective positions so often adopted by writers on such an emotive topic.

Many teachers expressed their anxieties about so-called 'revisionist' writings and political activities (outside schools, at football grounds, rock concerts, etc.). It is certainly undeniable that in the hands of a few truly malevolent individuals the subject of the Holocaust has been drawn into the spotlight purely so that its truthfulness can be manipulated and denied. Far from constituting a serious analysis of the Holocaust, such 'revisionist' history serves more as an example of the kind of twisted thinking that actually contributed to the Nazi horrors in the first place. With reference to such 'historians', Michael Marrus has written with appropriate contempt in the preface to his work *The Holocaust in History*: 'I see no reason why such people should set the agenda for the subject, any more than flat-earth theorists should set the agenda for astronomers.'

My own approach while preparing this book and weighing the views of the teachers who responded along these lines is that the most effective ways of countering the potentially harmful influence of Holocaust deniers, downplayers and other assorted categories within the 'revisionist' spectrum are to keep in mind the following: that care should be taken not to dignify their opinions, accusations and assertions with too many explicit acknowledgements or references (any more than Marrus' aforementioned 'flat-earth theorists' are allowed to set *his* agenda). In other words, it is quite unnecessary and probably counter-productive to write a book, teach a class or deliver a lecture with the *express* purpose of refuting their work; a corollary of this is that every serious word that *is* written or uttered on this subject is *implicitly* working counter to the revisionists' aims and desires. In short, while we should keep the problem posed by the revisionists at the forefront of our consciousness, we should guard against exaggerating its significance and thus providing the very publicity they seek, recognizing that there is usually a difference between the scholastic and the political arenas (they may overlap, but they are rarely identical).

The teachers interviewed were virtually unanimous that Jewish history in general and the Holocaust in particular must be taught in order to combat racial prejudice and the abuse of power. To fulfil this goal it was felt that, ideally, the Holocaust should not be torn from its historical and wider educational contexts – as so regularly happens – even if time is limited.

An enlightened and effective approach to understanding and transmitting awareness of the Holocaust can be built on the following philosophical and educational assumptions which can be adapted to most subjects and settings:

1 The Holocaust was an event that was *both* unique and universal, of far-reaching significance for the Jewish people but also with weighty, even mind-boggling, implications for us all.
2 The story of the Holocaust is potentially the ultimate 'humanities' topic; if taught skilfully and responsibly it can help socialize and even 'civilize' our students. But, if taught badly, it can titillate, traumatize, mythologize and encourage a purely negative view of all Jewish history, of Jewish people and, indeed, of *all* victim groups.
3 The Holocaust and its lessons should be approached within the following contexts:
   (a) Jewish history and the history of antisemitism;
   (b) modern German history;
   (c) 'genocide' in the nineteenth and twentieth centuries;
   (d) the misuse of technology and bureaucracy in the twentieth century; and
   (e) the psychology of human prejudice and racism.
4 The study of the Jewish historical experience, including that of the Holocaust, can serve as a highly effective educational means for sensitizing students to the distinct problem of antisemitism; to the universal issues of minority status and minority identities; to the need most of us have for cultural and national pride; and to the dangers of racial and religious stereotyping, prejudice and hatred.
5 The teacher and student of the Holocaust must try to reconcile the intimidating demands of the subject content with their own changing experience, values and awareness and, inescapably, those of the society and the times in which they live.
6 No one incident or experience can adequately convey the totality and magnitude of the Holocaust. This catastrophe was comprised of all kinds of components, each adding a horrifying dimension to the whole. Neither Kovno nor Treblinka, neither Wannsee nor Babi Yar can alone represent the others. It is collectively that they express the very worst that human beings can do to each other and to themselves.

PART I

READINGS AND EXERCISES

Note: Material in each section is intended for reading, reflection and class discussion.

NORWAY
82 years

ESTONIA
600 years

LATVIA
400 years

DENMARK
311 years

HOLLAND
800 years

BELGIUM
700 years

MEMEL
269 years

LITHUANIA
600 years

WHITE RUSSIA
550 years

GERMANY
1,612 years

DANZIG
400 years

Wlodawa

POLAND
800 years

UKRAINE
816 years

LUXEMBOURG
647 years

SAAR
312 years

CZECHOSLOVAKIA
1,000 years

AUSTRIA
1,030 years

HUNGARY
1,900 years

CRIMEA
1,900 years

FRANCE
1,930 years

ITALY
2,100 years

RUMANIA
1,800 years

YUGOSLAVIA
1,000 years

BULGARIA
1,900 years

GREECE
2,233 years

RHODES
2,000 years

miles   300

kilometres   400

© Martin Gilbert 1982

1   Two thousand years of Jewish life in Europe by 1933

The Holocaust – the futility of definition?

In his foreword to Yehuda Bauer's *The Jewish Emergence from Powerlessness* (Toronto University Press, 1979), the philosopher Emil Fackenheim included the following provocative piece. Read it carefully and discuss, or reflect upon, the acceptability of each of his assertions.

What was the Nazi Holocaust? So uncomprehended and incomprehensible is the dread event still, a whole generation after, that in this brief space we can answer this question only with a series of negations.

1. The Holocaust was not a war. Like all wars, the Roman War against the Jews was over conflicting interests – territorial, imperial, religious, other – waged between parties endowed, however unequally, with power. The victims of the Holocaust had no power. And they were a threat to the Third Reich only in the Nazi mind.
2. The Holocaust was not part of a war, a war crime. War crimes belong intrinsically to wars, whether they are calculated to further war goals, or are the result of passions that wars unleash. The Holocaust hindered rather than furthered the German war aims in World War II. And it was directed, not by passions but rather by a plan conceived and executed with methodical care, devoid of passion and, indeed, unable to afford this luxury.
3. The Holocaust was not a case of racism although, of course, the Nazis were racists. But they were racists because they were antisemites, not antisemites because they were racists (the case of the Japanese as honorary Aryans would suffice to bear this out). Racism asserts that some human groups are inferior to others, destined to slavery. The Holocaust enacted the principle that Jews are not of the human race at all but 'vermin' to be 'exterminated'.
4. The Holocaust was not a case of 'genocide' although it was in response to this crime that the world invented the term. Genocide is a modern phenomenon; for the most part in ancient times human beings were considered valuable, and were carried off into slavery. The genocides of modern history spring from motives, human, if evil, such as greed, hatred, or simply blind xenophobic passion. This is true even when they masquerade under high-flown ideologies. The Nazi genocide of the Jewish people did not masquerade under an ideology. The ideology was genuinely believed. This was an 'idealistic' genocide to which

war aims were, therefore, sacrificed. The ideal was to rid the world of Jews as one rids oneself of lice. It was also, however, to 'punish' the Jews for their 'crime', and the crime in question was existence itself. Hitherto such a charge had been directed only at devils. Jews had now become devils as well as vermin. And there is but one thing that devils and vermin have in common: neither is human.

5. The Holocaust was not an episode within the Third Reich, a footnote for historians. In all other societies, however brutal, people are 'punished' for *doing*. In the Third Reich 'non-Aryans' were 'punished' for *being*. In all other societies – in pretended or actual principle, if assuredly not always in practice – people are assumed innocent until proved guilty; the Nazi principle presumed every-one guilty until he had proved his 'Aryan' innocence. Hence anyone proving, or even prepared to prove, such innocence was implicated, however slightly and unwittingly, in the process which led to Auschwitz. The Holocaust is not an accidental by-product of the Reich but rather its inmost essence.

6. The Holocaust is not part of German history alone. It includes such as the Grand Mufti of Jerusalem, Haj Amin al-Husseini, who successfully urged the Nazi leaders to kill more Jews. It also includes all countries whose niggardly immigration policies prior to World War II cannot be explained in normal terms alone, such as the pressures of the Great Depression or a xenophobic tradition. Hitler did not wish to export national socialism but only antisemitism. He was widely successful. He succeeded when the world thought that 'the Jews' must have done *something* to arouse the treatment given them by a German government. He also succeeded when the world categorized Jews needing a refuge as 'useless people'. (In this category would have been Sigmund Freud had he still been in Austria rather than in England; Albert Einstein had he still been in Germany rather then America; . . . This was prior to the war. When the war had trapped the Jews of Nazi Europe, the railways to Auschwitz were not bombed. The Holocaust is not a parochial event. It is world-historical.

7. The Jews were no mere scapegoat in the Holocaust. It is true that they were used as such in the early stages of the Nazi movement. Thus Hitler was able to unite the 'left' and 'right' wings of his party by distinguishing, on the left, between 'Marxist' (i.e. Jewish) and 'national' (i.e. 'Aryan') 'socialism' and, on the right, between *raffendes Kapital* (rapacious, i.e. Jewish capital) and *schaffendes Kapital* (creative, i.e. 'Aryan' capital). It is also true that had the supply of Jewish victims given out Hitler would have been forced (as he once remarked to Hermann Rauschning) to 'invent' new 'Jews'. But it is not true that 'the Jew [was] . . . only a pretext' for something else. So long as there *were* actual Jews, it was these *actual* Jews who were the systematic object of ferreting-out, torture, and murder. Once, at Sinai, Jews had been singled out for life and a task. Now, at Auschwitz, they were singled out for torment and death.

8. The Holocaust is not over and done with. Late in the war Goebbels (who, needless to say, knew all) said publicly and with every sign of conviction that, among the peoples of Europe, the Jews alone had neither sacrificed nor

suffered in the war but only profited from it. As this was written, an American professor has written a book asserting that the Holocaust never happened, while other Nazis are preparing to march in Skokie [in Illinois, USA], in an assault on Jewish survivors. Like the old Nazis, the new Nazis say two things at once. The Holocaust never happened; and it is necessary to finish the job.

Obedience to authority 2

In the early 1960s a trailblazing, controversial and deeply disturbing series of experiments was conducted by the American psychologist, Stanley Milgram. He wanted to investigate patterns of obedience among 'ordinary' people in an attempt to understand, among other things, why so many Germans appeared to have obeyed orders unquestioningly – even when outrageous and immoral acts were asked of them. Milgram's results support the view that, even in our own 'normal' societies, we are very easily conditioned to respond positively to commands or requests from figures we think possess 'authority', even though we might know that such acts are wrong.

The following piece by Stanley Milgram comes from *TV Guide* (US), 21 August 1976.

Sometimes an event occurs during our lifetime that leaves an impression that is both indelible and puzzling. For me that event was the widespread participation of the German people in a system of death camps that destroyed millions of innocent men, women and children. The hapless victims were shot, gassed and burned in ovens.

These deeds were carried out by a people who were as civilized as any people in the world. How was it possible for them to act so cruelly? Did their behaviour reveal a potential that is present in all of us? As a social psychologist whose job is to look into the why and how of human behaviour, I decided to examine the response of ordinary people to immoral orders.

In order to explore behaviour, social psychologists often rely on an important tool, the experiment. Although experiments in chemistry and physics often involve shiny equipment, flasks and electronic gear, an experiment in social psychology smacks much more of dramaturgy or theatre. The experimenter carefully constructs a scenario to focus on certain aspects of behaviour, a scenario in which the end is unknown and is completed by the experimental subject. The psychologist tries to create circumstances that will allow him to look at the behaviour very carefully, note what he observed, and study its causes.

The experiment I set up was relatively simple: a person comes into the laboratory and, in the context of a learning experiment, he is told to give increasingly severe electric shocks to another person (who, unknown to the subject, is a confederate and does not actually receive the shocks). This arrangement gave me a chance to see how far people would go before they refused to follow the experimenter's orders. But a fuller scenario is needed to grasp the flavour of the experiment.

Imagine you had answered an advertisement to take part in a study of learning, and are arriving at the university at the time agreed upon. First, you are greeted by a man in grey technician's coat; he introduces you to a second volunteer and says you are both about to take part in a scientific experiment. He says it is to test whether the use of punishment improves the ability to learn.

You draw lots to see who is to be the teacher, and the other fellow the learner. Then you see the learner strapped into a chair and electrodes placed on his wrist. You are told that, when the learner makes a mistake in the lesson, his punishment will be an electric shock.

As teacher, you are seated in front of an impressive-looking instrument, a shock generator. Its essential feature is a line of switches that range from 15 volts to 450 volts, and a set of written labels that goes from slight shock to moderate shock, strong shock, very strong shock, and so on through XXX – danger, severe shock.

Your job, the experimenter explains to you, is to teach the learner a simple word-pair test. You read a list of words to him, such as blue day, nice girl, fat neck, etc., and he has to indicate by means of an answer box which words were originally paired together. If he gets a correct answer, you move on to the next pair. But if he makes a mistake, you are instructed to give him an electric shock starting with 15 volts. And you are told to increase the shock one step each time he makes an error. In the course of the experiment the 'victim' emits cries of pain and demands to be set free, but the experimenter orders you to continue. The question is: how far will you proceed on the shock generator before you turn to the experimenter and refuse to go on?

Before carrying out the experiment I wanted to know how people thought they would behave in this situation, and so I asked them to predict their own performance. I posed the question to several groups: psychiatrists, psychologists and ordinary workers. They all said virtually the same thing: almost no one would go to the end.

But in reality the results were very different. Despite the fact that many subjects experience stress, and protest to the experimenter, a substantial proportion continue to the last shock on the generator. Many subjects obeyed the experimenter no matter how vehement the pleading of the person being shocked, no matter how painful the shocks seemed to be, and no matter how much the victim pleaded to be let out. This was seen time and again in our studies and has been observed in several universities where the experiment has been repeated.

But there is more to the experiment than this simple demonstration of obedience. Most of our energy went into systematically changing the factors in this situation to see which ones increased obedience and which ones led to greater defiance. We studied the effects of the closeness of the victim, the importance of the sponsoring institution and how the sight of other people obeying or defying an authority affected obedience. All of these factors have a powerful effect on whether the subjects obeyed or defied the malevolent authority. This shows that how a person behaves depends not only on his 'character' but also on the precise situational pressures on him.

When the experiments were published, opinion about them was sharply divided. On the one hand, the American Association for the Advancement of Science awarded the work its annual socio-psychological prize. At the same time, the experiments attracted fierce criticism, centering mainly on the ethical issues of carrying out the research. The experiments that I had hoped would deepen our understanding of how people yield to authority became themselves the focus of controversy.

But the problem of authority remains. We cannot have society without some structure of authority, and every society must inculcate a habit of obedience in its citizens. Yet those experiments show that many people do not have the resources to resist authority, even when they are directed to act inhumanly against an innocent victim. The experiments pose anew the age-old problem: what is the correct balance between individual initiative and social authority? They illuminate in a concrete way what happens when obedience is unrestrained by conscience.

Source: Stanley Milgram in TV Guide *(US), 21 August 1976 quoted in* The Holocaust Years: Society on Trial *(B'nai B'rith Anti-Defamation League, 1979)*

Jewish powerlessness and 3
choicelessness

The following extract comes from Alexander Donat's extraordinary memoir, *The Holocaust Kingdom*. This excerpt describes a Nazi round-up in the Warsaw Ghetto, the mounting terror and impossible psychological conditions confronting Jews. At this early stage, the ghetto victims placed deceptive faith in documents (in this instance the *Ausweis* or identity card) as a guarantee of exemption from deportation.

I saw a young mother run downstairs into the street to get milk for her baby. Her husband, who worked at the 'Ostbahn', had as usual left earlier that morning. She had not bothered to dress, but was in bathrobe and slippers. An empty milk bottle in hand, she was headed for a shop where, she knew, they sold milk under the counter. She walked into Operation Reinhard. The executioners demanded her *Ausweis*. 'Upstairs . . . *Ostbahn* . . . work certificate. I'll bring it right away.'

'We've heard that one before. Have you got an *Ausweis* with you, or haven't you?'

She was dragged protesting to the wagon, scarcely able to realize what was happening. 'But my baby is all alone. Milk . . .' she protested. 'My *Ausweis* is upstairs.' Then, for the first time, she really looked at the men who were holding her and saw where she was being dragged: to the gaping entrance at the back of a high boarded wagon with victims already jammed into it. With all her young mother's strength, she wrenched herself free, and then two, and four policemen fell on her, hitting her, smashing her to the ground, picking her up again, and tossing her into the wagon like a sack. I can still hear her screaming in a half-crazed voice somewhere between a sob of utter human despair and the howl of an animal.

Another young woman I knew, after much trouble, finally persuaded a friend of her husband's, a man who managed a shop, to register her with his firm so that she could have an *Ausweis*. 'I'm doing it for you because you're Leon's wife,' the man told her, but it cost her every penny of what remained of the possessions she and her husband had owned when he had left in September 1939. 'You know I'm not taking this for myself. You understand, don't you? It's because of the others . . .' Then he explained to her how the very next day she must move to the shop area and bring her eight-year-old boy with her. There she would be safe. She needn't worry about having no money or about leaving her apartment; she must bring only the absolute necessities with her, no more than the apartment house janitor's wheelbarrow could carry in one trip; but everything would be all right.

And, indeed, she was reassured. Calmly, she went about doing what she had to do, fighting for the life of her child. Her husband, she knew, would be proud of how well she had managed. Holding her little boy's hand, she told him, 'Now, you mustn't be afraid. Mother is looking out for you.' As she was turning the corner into the street where they lived, the little boy ran ahead, as children do. He skipped around the corner before she got to it. Why had she let him do it? How could she have let her sense of danger relax even for an instant? The street seemed so calm. When she heard him scream, 'Mama! Mama!' she sped around the corner and had just time enough to see a little body with a familiar striped sweater disappearing among the mass of other bodies in the wagon surrounded by police. She thanked God that she was in time to explain, that she had an *Ausweis*.

'But Madam,' the police said, 'how can we be sure that this is your child?'

She had not, it seems, quite understood. No more than any of us did at first. And when she finally did understand, she was beaten brutally 'for resisting the authorities,' but not a sound, not a sob escaped her. The policeman showed that they were not, after all, completely heartless. By surrendering her *Ausweis* to them – a commodity more valuable than gold at that point – she was permitted to get into the wagon, too, to accompany her son to the *Umschlagplatz*, and what lay beyond.

As the wagon began to move away, anyone within earshot could hear the voice of an old woman coming from beyond the boards of the van, repeating monotonously, 'Tell Zalme Katz his mother was taken away . . . Tell Zalme Katz his mother was taken away.'

Source: Alexander Donat, The Holocaust Kingdom *(Holt, Rinehart and Wilson, 1965) quoted in Albert Friedlander (ed.),* Out of the Whirlwind: A Reader of Holocaust Literature *(Schocken Books, 1976) and in Margot Strom and William Parsons,* Facing History and Ourselves: Holocaust and Human Behaviour *(Intentional Educations Inc., 1982)*

The moral responsibility of 'ordinary' Germans 4

One of the most perplexing questions in one's study of the Holocaust concerns that of the German people's knowledge about, and apparent indifference towards, the persecution of the Jews in their midst. However, questions concerning the 'responsibility' of ordinary citizens whose governments commit terrible deeds in their name are extremely complex and debatable. To pass judgement on the moral conduct of others is often highly delicate, personal and prejudiced – all the more so when that behaviour takes place in a society and a context which are radically different from our own.

The following text is an experimental exercise to provide students with the opportunity to explore some of the most demanding moral questions raised by a study of the Holocaust. It comprises the transcript of 'trials' of two German defendants. Both of the characters are invented, but carefully drawn to represent the attitudes of sizeable numbers of real Germans during the Nazi era. What is being evaluated here is not so much their behaviour as the values and opinions that underlie their actions or, as is more appropriate in this instance, their inaction. These trials did not actually take place, nor, indeed, could they have taken place, for no one is put on trial for their moral attitudes. However, the significance of ordinary people's values in determining the outcome of the Holocaust – and, indeed, of many important historical events – should not be underestimated.

Recommendations for tutor

1 Each trial should be read dramatically, with one member of the class reading the prosecutor's questions, another the defendant's replies.
2 After each trial the class should silently read through the extra pieces

of information and suggested discussion questions provided. The class should then discuss the defendant's statements and moral position.

3 It is important to stress to the class that there is no additional information about the defendants other than that provided; that, unlike a real trial, it must be assumed that each defendant always tells the truth (i.e. honestly represents or recreates his feelings); and that the apparent absence of remorse should not, in this artificially constructed exercise, be counted against the defendants. What is on trial are their opinions and sentiments at the time, i.e. during the Hitler years.

4 The purpose of the trials is *not* to establish a simple verdict of innocent or guilty, as would be the case in a genuine criminal prosecution. The aim is to consider the *degree of moral responsibility* of each defendant.

5 When the case against the second defendant has been discussed, the class may, at the tutor's discretion, assign a score out of ten to each defendant, representing the degree to which they believe the defendant was 'morally responsible' for the plight and ultimate fate of the Jews (the higher the score the higher the degree of responsibility). Such a climax to the exercise is obviously subjective in the extreme and has the educational merit of allowing the students to compare their value judgements with those of their fellow-students in a way that is concrete, challenging and visible.

THE TRIALS

The case against Hans Brenner

In the mid-1930s, Hans Brenner had started to work in a munitions plant near Munich. This was the first time he had had a good job. Until then things had been extremely difficult economically for him and his family. But now he could afford a decent home, to raise his family in some kind of security. Neither he nor his wife participated in any political activities.

P = Prosecutor
D = Defendant

P: Your wife has told us much about your family. I am curious, Hans, when you began working for the munitions factory, what were conditions like?

D: For me, they were good. I had little training or experience, so I was thankful for the job.

P: What was your job at the plant?

D: I had several. First, I had to learn, so they put me under some specialists to teach me about electro-welding. I worked as an apprentice for a long time.

P: Who were the specialists?

D: Some of them were Jews.

P: Jews?

D: Yes, there many Jews working in the plant.

P: Where did they come from?

D: There were camps close by . . . They would come from these camps.

P: Did you get along with them?

D: I learned my job from them, that's all. I did not speak to them nor spend time with them. It was difficult enough that I had to learn from them.

P: Were they unkind?

D: They were Jews. It was ironic that I should be learning from a Jew. I should have been teaching them a thing or two.

P: They were better skilled than you . . .

D: That is because they had better opportunities than I had to learn. They had all the advantages that I never had . . .

P: You, nevertheless, learned the skills, didn't you?

D: Oh yes, I was a good student. I soon became the supervisor of the electro-welding shop. It was good pay.

P: What happened to those Jews who taught you your skills?

D: Many of them stayed on at the plant . . . Some of them were sent away to deportation centres.

P: Those who stayed on, did they work for you?

D: Of course, I was their supervisor. You must understand, however, I was only their supervisor at the plant.

P: What were your responsibilities to them?

D: I had none to them. My only concern was that our production quota be met. If a worker failed to meet the quota, he was reported.

P: What happened to those workers?

D: They did not return to work. I do not know what happened to them . . .

P: What were the working conditions like at your plant?

D: For us, it was good. There were opportunities for us to rest during the day. We were paid well. The working conditions for Jews were different. You must understand, they were regarded as enemies of the people. They were carefully watched and had to work without rest. We had to work them very hard for many hours. When the work was done for the day, an SS soldier would line them up and march them back to the camp. No, I would not have liked to be one of them.

P: Tell me about the Jews at your plant. What did they look like? How did they behave themselves?

D: They were like robots . . . They did not speak . . . They only worked. What else can I say? They were different. They were from Hungary, Poland, Rumania and so forth. They looked like they were starving . . .

P: Did you talk to them?

D: Only when absolutely necessary.

P: Were they fed during the day at the plant?

D: They had no break for lunch. We were told they were fed before work at the camp . . .

P: Did you make any effort to investigate whether they were fed?

D: That was none of my business . . .

P: Did any of them die at the plant?

D: I personally did not see any of them die. Some of them collapsed on the job and were carried away. I do not know whether they died or not . . . they may have. All I know, they did not return to work the next day.

P: Tell me, Hans, how were you paid? What determined how much you would be paid?

D: We were paid a salary and we received a bonus . . .

P: Was this bonus determined by the amount the individual exceeded his quota?

D: Oh, no, we worked as a team. If a section exceeded the quota, then all the workers in the section received the same bonus.

P: With the exception of the Jews?

D: They received no pay for their work . . .

P: Yet they contributed greatly through their work to your receiving a bonus?

D: Of course. We were a section.

P: Didn't you feel some guilt that you were receiving bonuses for their labour and that they received nothing?

D: Why should I? There was nothing I could do about it. If the Jews did not receive pay for their work, that was their problem. If they did not work hard, then it was our problem, because our bonuses would be less. We were all concerned about work . . . for different reasons. You asked if I felt guilty . . . My answer is no. It was not my fault that they were there. If I did not receive a bonus, then my family would do without, then that would be my fault. The Jew and the German both profited by hard work. The German received a bonus, the Jew stayed alive.

Information

Read the following.

1 Hans Brenner's feelings towards the Jews at his plant were influenced by Nazi propaganda which, in turn, fed on the historic hatred of the Jews in Germany dating back to the time of Martin Luther and beyond. At the end of the nineteenth century, the German Chancellor, Von Caprivi, summed up antisemitism with the following words: 'The movement now introduced in Germany is widely spread, already beyond the welfare of the state. Passions have been evoked that may be impossible to channel.'

2 The Jews were generally viewed with suspicion. The following quotations from Hitler's *Mein Kampf* became the official attitude of the Nazis towards the Jews:

The Jews have no civilization of their own and, therefore, are bent on destroying all other civilizations . . . For this purpose they dominate the press, high finance and the trades unions . . . They corrupt literature and the arts . . . I enjoin the government and the people to uphold the racial laws and to limit and mercilessly resist international Jewry, the poisoner of all nations.

3 In spite of severe discrimination against the Jews, the Germans had great need for them during the early years of the rise of the Third Reich. By 1941, tens of thousands of Jews had become forced labourers in the armaments industry. Many labour camps were purposefully constructed near industrial centres so that they could employ Jewish labour. In some cases, industries were moved near large concentration camps. Many Jews from surrounding countries were imported to work in German industries as slave labourers.

4 Hans Brenner was thankful for the opportunity of being employed. The economic growth of Germany following the rise of Hitler was phenomenal. Unemployment, the curse of the 1920s and 1930s, was reduced from over six million in 1932, to less than one million by 1940. The national income was doubled.

5 The basis of Germany's recovery was rearmament. The whole German economy was known as a war economy, and it was deliberately designed to function not only in time of war but even during the 'peace' that came before the war.

6 Receiving additional income by increased production was a basic tenet of Hitler. 'It has become an iron principle of the National Socialist leadership', he declared early in his regime, 'not to permit any rise in the hourly wage rate, but to raise income solely by the increase in performance.' In a country where most wages were based, at least partly, on piecework, this meant that a worker could hope to earn more only by speeding up and by longer hours. The general wage level for the German worker was low: barely enough to meet minimal needs.

Discussion questions

Consider the following questions while you discuss the case against Hans Brenner. What contemporary or universal issues are raised by these questions?

1 Hans Brenner justified his attitudes towards the Jews on the basis of his previous lack of opportunity. Do individuals and groups have the right to demand certain benefits today because of past inequities they have suffered? Can you think of examples where this has happened, or still happens?

2 Is it realistic to expect Hans Brenner to act differently towards the Jews in the light of his personal needs for income and security?

3 Hans Brenner gained his bonuses from the labour of others. Is this basically a crime? Is it in your view immoral? Does this condition prevail

in your own country? In what ways are the circumstances similar and in what ways different?

4 Have you yourself ever been the victim of discrimination because of religious, racial, national, political or other affiliations? Have you ever been guilty of such discrimination against others? Consider the circumstances of such examples.

The case against Dr Ernst Schmid

P = Prosecutor
D = Defendant

P: Dr Schmid, what is your profession?

D: I am a minister of the Lutheran Church.

P: What was the status of your church during the period of Hitler?

D: That is a difficult question. The status of my Church was no different from any other denomination. Our churches were allowed to exist. We were given no special favours.

P: Your Church was the principal religious denomination of Germany at that time . . . ?

D: It was, and still is. Germany experienced the beginning of the Lutheran Church. Martin Luther was German. There are really two principal religions in Germany: Catholicism and Lutheranism.

P: And these two religions were able to live with each other without conflict?

D: There has always been some kind of conflict between the German Catholics and the Lutherans. Before Hitler, Germany was divided. Religious and political rivalry created serious problems in our country.

P: You are implying that Hitler was able to resolve this conflict?

D: Not entirely. Hitler did bring about unity through his National Socialist programmes. The Germans were finally able to work together for a national purpose, Lutheran and Catholic alike. Our religious differences were still there, but were of lesser importance than our national purposes.

P: Rev. Schmid, what did you do to help save the Jews during the Holocaust?

D: My knowledge of the Holocaust, that is, the destruction of the Jews in such a hideous way, didn't really come about until 1944, when it was too late to do anything. If I would have known that this was going to happen to the Jews, maybe I could have done something during the early years of the war. We did help other refugees by giving them food . . . some shelter. We did a great deal for them. They were principally Germans who lost their homes because of the war. Many were children who lost their families.

P: Is is possible that among the refugees there could have been some Jews?

D: It is possible at first. We didn't ask the religion of those we helped. Later on, but still in the early years, we could identify the Jews by the badges they wore on their sleeves. There were a few who came to us for help.

P: Had there been more, would you have helped them?

D: That is a difficult question. If we were discovered helping Jews, we would have been punished ourselves. Our work in helping the other refugees took priority over helping those few Jews who came to us. Our existence would have been placed in jeopardy. We had to decide whether we should deny assistance to a few for the sake of many.

P: You did save many lives?

D: Thousands. But remember, this could only have been done with the assistance of the government. They provided much of the needed supplies for us to be of service to the refugees. We had to cooperate with them. We had to conform to their wishes.

P: Rev. Schmid, before the war, when you first began your ministry, did you see any signs of what was about to happen to the Jews?

D: No one could predict what was about to happen to the Jews. The treatment of the Jews was really not much different from before. There had always been hostile feelings towards the Jews. The government's position towards the Jews was no different from that of most of the people.

P: Did you personally see any real signs of antisemitism in your country?

D: I had read of some burning of Jewish stores. On one occasion, I saw a synagogue put to flames. You must understand that this was nothing new in Germany. These kinds of thing happen ... even in your country. It was expected to happen to the Jew.

P: Why the Jew?

D: I suppose it has always happened to him. There has been a great deal of superstition about the Jews that dates back to the period of Christ. Much is written about the Jew as the Anti-Christ.

P: How could you, as a clergyman, allow the persecution of the Jews to take place?

D: It was written that they should suffer. Not the total death, not the Holocaust, perhaps, but the Jews could have avoided much of the persecution. The Church allows conversions, regardless of one's previous religion. As long as one remains a Jew, then it is his choice to suffer.

P: But you, as a human being ... how could you allow this to happen?

D: The decision was theirs. They could have come to the Church for salvation. They did not need to go through the torture.

P: Didn't it become too late for them even if they wanted to convert?

D: Yes, when finally the Nazis took over the idealism of the Church and perverted it to their racial superiority concepts, the Jews were doomed. Even those who came to us for conversion ...

P: When this idea of racial superiority took over and all Jews were considered inferior and needed to be destroyed, what did you do? It was no longer their fault that they were not Christians. What did you do?

D: I had to save the lives of the majority ... I had no other choice.

P: So, you allowed the Jews to be exterminated?

D: Persecuted, not exterminated. I did not see them exterminated.
P: But, six million died.
D: I was not a witness.

Information

Read the following.

1 Some commentators have interpreted the extermination of the Jews as a logical conclusion to a 2,000 year tradition of antisemitism initiated at the birth of Christianity. The Christian view of the Jew, as preached to the masses for centuries, formed the basis of the anti-Jewish Nazi propaganda which was so readily accepted by the majority of the populace.

2 The Christian Church wanted to protect itself from Jewish teachings and the allegedly harmful consequences of contact with the Jews. Historic Christianity would not tolerate the Jew in its midst. The Jew who would not convert was often expelled from one Christian country or another.

3 Martin Luther, at the time of the Reformation, said this about the Jew: 'Jews hold us captive in our country. The Jews are like a plague, pure misfortune for our country.'

4 In the Gospel according to St Paul, Jews are represented as the murderers of God; the sacrificial death was preordained; God, the Father, had willed it and had blinded the Jews in order to bring it about. The Jews were to bear this curse until the end of time. Augustine decried the role of the Jews in the Christian world. Other Christian fathers and scholars, Thomas Aquinas for one, reiterated: 'Like Cain, the Jews must not be destroyed. They must be preserved forever to serve as witnesses of the Christian faith; they must live as *perpetual servants* to the Christian people.'

5 The relentless hostility of the early Christian Church was the basis of subsequent anti-Judaism. All persecutions, restrictions, exclusions (economic, social, political), all degradation and humiliation which the Jews underwent in the western world, may be traced to this Christian attitude towards Judaism which spread with the expanding power of the Church.

6 For centuries the Church held the Jews responsible for the death of Jesus. Bishop Gilmours, a prominent leader in the Lutheran Church in the 1930s, stated: 'The blood of Christ has been upon the Jews, who were driven from Judea and have been without a country and home, strangers among strangers, wandering from nation to nation bearing with them the visible sign of God's curse, hated yet feared.'

Discussion questions

Consider the following questions while you discuss the case against Ernst Schmid. What contemporary and universal issues are raised by these questions?

1 Is Ernst Schmid an inescapable carrier of the teachings of his own Church? If so, to what extent can he be held responsible for his attitudes?

2 Is it right to demand higher moral standards of clergymen, not only during the Nazi era but in own societies?

3 How much validity do you attach to the claim that he could only save selectively?

4 What, in your view, are the similarities and the differences between religious bigotry and racial prejudice?

5 What stereotypes exist in your own society about members of different religious groups? Do you feel such stereotypes to be harmful or innocuous?

Source: Adapted from materials produced by Alternatives in Religious Education, Denver, Colorado. Reprinted by permission of A.R.E. Publishing, Inc. from The Holocaust: A Study in Values *by Raymond A. Zwerin, Audrey Friedman Marcus, and Leonard Kramish. Copyright by A.R.E. Publishing, Inc., 1976*

Six million accusers 5

An excerpt from the speech of Gideon Hausner, Chief Prosecutor at the trial of Adolf Eichmann, 1961. Eichmann was the Nazi bureaucrat responsible for organizing the deportations of the Jews to the death camps.

When I stand before you here, Judges of Israel, to lead the Prosecution of Adolf Eichmann, I am not standing alone. With me are six million accusers. But they cannot rise to their feet and point an accusing finger towards him who sits in the dock and cry: 'I accuse.' For their ashes are piled up on the hills of Auschwitz and the fields of Treblinka, and are strewn in the forests of Poland. Their graves are scattered throughout the length and breadth of Europe. Their blood cries out, but their voice is not heard. Therefore I will be their spokesman and in their name I will unfold the awesome indictment.

The history of the Jewish people is steeped in suffering and tears . . . Yet never, down the entire blood-stained road travelled by this people, never since the first days of its nationhood, has any man arisen who succeeded in dealing it such grievous blows as did Hitler's iniquitous regime, and Adolf Eichmann as its executive arm for the extermination of the Jewish people. In all human history there is no other example of a man against whom it would be possible to draw up a bill of indictment as has been read here . . . Murder has been with the human race since the days when Cain killed Abel: it is no novel phenomenon. But we have had to wait till this twentieth century to witness with our own eyes a new kind of murder: not the result of a momentary surge of passion or mental blackout, but of calculated decision and painstaking planning; not through the evil design of an individual, but through a mighty criminal conspiracy involving thousands; not against one victim whom an assassin may have decided to destroy, but against an entire people . . .

This murderous decision, taken deliberately and in cold blood, to annihilate a nation and blot it out from the face of the earth, is so shocking that one is at a loss for words to describe it. Words exist to express what man's reason can conceive and his heart contain, [but] here we are dealing with actions that transcend our human grasp. Yet this is what did happen; millions were condemned to death, not for any crime, not for anything they had done, but only because they belonged to the Jewish people. The development of technology placed at the disposal of the destroyers efficient equipment for the execution of their appalling designs. This unprecedented crime, carried out by Europeans in the twentieth century, led to the definition of a criminal concept unknown to human annals even during the darkest ages – the crime of Genocide . . .

Hitler, his regime and crimes, was no accidental or transient phenomenon. He did not come to power as a result merely of a unique combination of circumstances. Historical processes are usually the product of many developments, like many streams flowing each into its own channel until they combine into a mighty river. They will come together only if their flow is in the same general direction.

No doubt various events contributed to the rise of Nazism: the defeat of Germany in World War I; the subsequent economic difficulties; lack of leadership and futile party divisions; fratricidal strife and disunion – all these impelled the German people, disoriented and groping, to turn its eyes towards the false prophet. But Hitler would not have been able to remain in power, and to consolidate in his support all the strata of the German people, including most of the intellectuals – to win the support of so many university professors and professional men, the civil service and the whole army – if the road to his leadership had not already been paved. Not even the oppressive regime of the concentration camps, and the atmosphere created by the terror so rapidly activated against all opposition by the hooligans of the SS and SA, are adequate alone to explain the enthusiastic and devoted support he received from the majority of the nation, unless it had been preceded by an extensive spiritual preparation. When we read today the declaration of the scientists, authors and journalists – including many who had not been among his adherents before – who chanted his praises and willingly gave him their support and backing, how they willingly and joyfully accepted his yoke, we must reach the conclusion, however reluctantly, that the people were ready and prepared to crown him as their leader.

Hitler [freed] the hatred of the Jew which was latent in the hearts of large sections of the German people, intensified it and stimulated it into greater activity. The germ of antisemitism was already there; he stimulated it and transformed it into the source of an epidemic. For the purposes of Nazi Germany's internal policy, the Jew was a convenient object of hatred; he was weak and defenceless. The world outside remained silent when he was persecuted, and contented itself with verbal reactions that did little harm. The Jew was pilloried as a supporter of Communism – and therefore an enemy of the German people. In the same breath he was accused of being a capitalist – and therefore an enemy of the workers. National-Socialism had found in the Jew an object of hostility appropriate to both halves of its name, and it set him up as a target for both national enmity and class hatred. The Jew was also a ready target through which the attention of the public could be diverted from other problems. This was an age-old weapon, which had been used by many antisemites down the ages . . .

A confused and blinded world was not alarmed by the campaign of hatred and the denial of human rights. It did not understand that the persecution of the Jews was only the beginning of an onslaught on the entire world. The man whose henchmen howled the infamous words: 'When Jewish blood spurts from the knife/ Then all goes doubly well!' ('*Wenn Judenblut vom Messer spritzt/ Dann geht's nochmal so gut!*') – the same man would soon, by a natural development and led by the same master-feeling of hate, proclaim that all the cities of England would be subjected to the same fate as bombed Coventry.

In order to complete the picture, we should point out that there were in Germany tens of thousands of scientists and ecclesiastics, statesmen and authors and ordinary people, who dared to help the Jews, to raise their heads in opposition to the iniquitous regime, and even to rebel against it, and among these were men whose names were famous in German science and culture. Thousands of opponents of the bloody regime were imprisoned and were later destined to suffer greatly in concentration camps before the Nazi monster was brought low. Thousands of these died without seeing the day of liberation. Hundreds of ecclesiastics were arrested and imprisoned. There were also examples of personal bravery – like that of a priest who was sent by Eichmann to a concentration camp for intervening openly on behalf of the Jews. There were Germans who hid Jews and shared their rations with them and who at the risk of their own lives helped them to hide or to obtain 'Aryan' papers, and there were others who maintained an anti-Hitler underground. During the war there were Germans who even protested to Hitler at the disgrace the Gestapo was bringing on the German people by acting like beasts of prey, as they described the extermination of the Jews. There were also soldiers who tried to frustrate the killings by direct intervention.

But after all is said and done, these were a very small minority. The decisive majority of the German people made peace with the new regime, and were phlegmatic witnesses of the most terrible crime ever perpetrated in human history . . .

There is a Hebrew saying: 'The wicked, even at the gate of Hell, do not repent.' In April 1945, at the moment of his death agonies, when the Soviet cannons were thundering in the streets of Berlin, when Hitler sat imprisoned in the cellar of his *Reichskanzlei*, his entire world in ruins and his country stricken, over the corpses of six million Jews – at that moment, the Führer wrote his last will and testament. He bequeathed to his people the injunction of eternal hatred for the Jews, and he concluded:

Above all, I enjoin the government and the people to uphold the racial laws to the limit and to resist mercilessly the poisoner of all nations, international Jewry.

Even from beyond the grave, Hitler was trying to sow the seeds of hatred and destruction for the Jewish people.

Source: Shabatai Rosenne (ed.), Six Million Accusers: Israel's Case Against Eichmann *(The Jerusalem Post, 1961), pp. 29–33, 37–38, 43. Reproduced in Paul Mendes-Flohr and Jehuda Reinharz (eds),* The Jew in the Modern World *(Oxford University Press, 1980)*

6 Euphemisms of death: Interpreting a primary source document on the Holocaust

by Richard Kalfus

The van's load is usually nine per square yard. In Saurer vehicles, which are very spacious, maximum use of space is impossible, not because of any possible overload, but because loading to full capacity would affect the vehicle's stability. So reduction of the load space seems necessary. It must absolutely be reduced by a yard, instead of trying to solve the problem, as hitherto, by reducing the number of pieces loaded. Besides, this extends the operating time, as the empty void must also be filled with carbon monoxide. On the other hand, if the load space is reduced, and the vehicle is packed solid, the operating time can be considerably shortened. The manufacturers told us during a discussion that reducing the size of the van's rear would throw it badly off balance. The front axle, they claim, would be overloaded. In fact, the balance is automatically restored, because the merchandise aboard displays during the operation a natural tendency to rush to the rear doors, and is mainly found lying there at the end of the operation. So the front axle is not overloaded.

The lighting must be better protected than now. The lamps must be enclosed in a steel grid to prevent their being damaged. Lights could be eliminated, since they apparently are never used. However, it has been observed that when the doors are shut, the load always presses hard against them [against the doors] as soon as darkness sets in. This is because the load naturally rushes towards the light when darkness sets in, which makes closing the doors difficult. Also, because of the alarming nature of darkness, screaming always occurs when the doors are closed. It would therefore be useful to light the lamps before and during the first moments of the operation.

For easy cleaning of the vehicle, there must be a sealed drain in the middle of the floor. The drainage hole's cover, eight to twelve inches in diameter, would be equipped with a slanting trap, so that fluid liquids can drain off during the operation. During cleaning, the drain can sometimes be used to evacuate large pieces of dirt.

The aforementioned technical changes are to be made to vehicles in service only when they come in for repairs. As for the ten vehicles ordered from Saurer, they must be equipped with all innovations and changes shown by use and experience to be necessary.[1]

After teaching about the Holocaust for more than ten years, I have found one document which more than any other source illustrates the all-pervasive, destructive force that was National Socialism. The insidious, administrative language used here is a concrete, dramatic example of how an entire caste of civil servants could become active participants in the extermination process.

We have before us a business memorandum, outlining specific technical problems and a suggested solution. The stability of a vehicle, a van, is in question. The primary issue is a need for maximum efficiency. What are the alternatives? If the load space is left as it is and the 'pieces' to be loaded are reduced, then the operating time would be longer, for the empty space (void) has to be filled with carbon monoxide; but if the load space (the size of the van) is reduced by a yard and the vehicle packed solid, then the operating time would be shortened, while still ensuring the van's stability. Note what is important to the writer of the memo: efficient use of time (operating time). The job of loading the pieces has to be accomplished quickly and efficiently but without damaging the lamps or the van itself by unnecessary soiling. Cleaning of the van, for example, during and after the operation is a major concern.

The objective and dispassionate language of a business memo depicts the helplessness and passivity of the victims: the merchandise and the pieces are the Jews. A state of being verb ('is') and a past participle are repeatedly used; a bureaucratic 'must-tone' (this has to be taken care of now!) is further articulated through the helping verb 'must'; everything is being done and has to be done TO the merchandise or pieces:

1 It (the load space) must be absolutely reduced.
2 The empty void must also be filled.
3 The vehicle is packed solid.
4 Merchandise – is mainly found lying.
5 Lighting must be better protected.
6 Lamps must be enclosed.
7 Technical changes are to be made.

The ultimate irony in this document is that the writer is betrayed by the very language he so carefully chooses. It is as if certain words have a life of their own. Let us look at the following three lines: 'the merchandise aboard displays . . . a natural tendency to rush to the rear doors'; 'the load always presses hard against them' and 'the load naturally rushes towards the light'. Action verbs are used as if one were speaking of human beings (displays, presses, rushes) yet the reference is to merchandise and the load. One notices how illogical this all sounds when the writer speaks of the load's 'natural' tendency to rush or how it 'naturally' rushes towards the light. Can one then be speaking about inanimate objects? Further doubt and a grotesque dimension is added in the following line: 'screaming always occurs when the doors are closed'. The memo's business as usual tone of objectivity is suddenly suspended. This verbal noun, denoting the most human of actions, has as its antecedent the word 'load'. Can a load scream? – is a logical question which the reader must ask himself. Raul Hilberg poignantly describes the blatant use of such euphemisms by the Nazis: 'the key to successful transportation of the Jews to death and extermination from a psychological standpoint was never to utter the words that would be appropriate to the actions being taken'.[2]

An excellent follow-up class activity to a general discussion of the memorandum is a small group analysis of the text in which students are asked to replace the euphemisms of the passage with their intended meaning: 'merchandise', 'pieces' and 'load' become the Jews; 'operating time' becomes annihilation; 'operation' becomes gassing; and most grotesque and repulsive of all – the 'fluid liquids' become urine and 'pieces of dirt' become human excrement. Students are asked in their respective groups to express to one another how they *feel* after the text has been decoded. Here, there is a dynamic, emotional aspect which I strongly believe can help students grasp this absurd, yet all too real, element of life in Nazi Germany. It is important, at this juncture, to point out to students that the terminology of the memo is consistent with the imagery so often employed by Hitler in *Mein Kampf* which describes the Jews as bacteria and vermin worthy of annihilation. The learning experience, of having one student from a group reread the document to the class *after* the euphemisms have been replaced, is an emotionally powerful one. It is one thing to read the memo silently; it is quite another matter to hear this Nazi voice of death without its euphemistic cover-up resonate grotesquely in the classroom.

It is only at this point that I present to the class the following brief introduction which accompanied the original memo. The euphemisms of the text have an even greater impact on students when they read:

Geheime Reichssache [Secret Reich Business]
Berlin, June 5, 1942

Changes for special vehicles now in service at Kulmhof (Chelmno) and for those now being built.

Since December 1941, ninety-seven thousand have been processed [*verarbeitet* in German] by the three vehicles in service, with no major incidents. In the light of observations made so far, however, the following technical changes are needed.[3]

Like meat at a slaughterhouse, **97,000** have been processed in six months. There is no direct reference to human beings. The German *verarbeitet* is a common word used, for example, in the context of forming or kneading dough into bread or cake. Thus, the victim appears as a helpless mass in the hands of a brutal executioner.

There are no compromises when efficient time management is a major objective: technical changes are made to vehicles in service *only* when they come in for repairs. Any interruption in the gassing process must be avoided. This type of technocratic mentality, devoid of all moral checks, was once defined by sociologists Max Weber and Karl Mannheim as functional rationality: 'it is concerned with long-range results but with cost effectiveness ... It is indeed, necessary for the purposes of functional rationality to accomplish the reduction of human beings to the status of things, in order that the efficiency of the whole process not be impaired by the irrelevances of humane considerations. NOTHING must interfere with the neat surgical precision of the process of completing the assigned task.'[4]

In studying the Holocaust, we discover that not only the Jewish victims had to become objects, but the Nazi perpetrators as well. The entire process of gas van killing was a symbol of grotesque, tragic irony. One of the very reasons for employing gas vans for extermination in Russia and later in the concentration camp at Chelmno, Poland was to 'depersonalize' the killing of Jews: mass shootings in front of open pits had become too subjective and emotional an experience for the special SS commandos (*Einsatzgruppen*).

SS officer Walther Rauff, head of the office of technical affairs in charge of more than 4,000 security police motor vehicles, was the bureaucrat to whom this memo was addressed. Rauff is our functional rationalist par excellence: 'The firing squads in Russia suffered frequent nervous breakdowns and need a more humane method of killing.'[5] The gas vans became, in late autumn 1941, the 'more humane method' of killing the Jews.[6] With this kind of attitude well established, it is not difficult to see how another bureaucrat, Willy Just, a dispatcher and welder for the SS motor pool, could have written the document under discussion, without one direct reference to the Jewish victim. He too had become a mere object, a calculating instrument of destruction with whom human considerations played no role.

Rauff's comment or Just's memo to him were not isolated, atypical utterances by insane individuals: they were features of a system which set as its goal the annihilation of the Jews. Take for example the following memorandum excerpt written in July 1941, about six months prior to the period of full-scale deployment of gas vans at Chelmno. SS Major Rolf-Heinz Hoppner, assigned to the Lodz ghetto, from where most of the Jews

were transported to Chelmno, writes to Adolf Eichmann, the SS officer
responsible for Jewish deportation from all over Europe:

> This winter there is a danger that not all the Jews can be fed any
> more. One should weigh honestly if the most humane solution
> might not be to finish off those of the Jews who are not employ-
> able by means of some quick-working device. At any rate, that
> would be more pleasant than to let them starve to death.[7]

Once again the Jewish victim is perceived as an animal to be put out of its
misery – to be 'finished off', like a horse with a broken leg, by a kind master.

The gas van operation at Chelmno was an efficiently run business.
Heinrich Himmler, the Head of the SS, was the 'company' chief executive
officer who wanted the best available men to complete successfully the task
of mass extermination. He employed, for example, many of the scientists
and administrative experts who supervised the murder of more than 50,000
mentally and physically handicapped Germans during the euthanasia
programme of 1939/40. A Nazi administrator's success was always measured
in terms of the number of prisoners transported and killed. When Eichmann,
for example, talks about his job, we get a clear and terrifying sense of the
reverse morality code which motivated Nazi behaviour:

> I did not take on the job as a senseless exercise. It gave me uncommon
> joy. I found it fascinating to have to deal with these matters . . .
> My job was to catch these enemies and transport them to their
> destination . . . I lived in this stuff, otherwise I would have remained
> only an assistant, a cog, something soulless.[8]

Whoever heard that someone's very soul was dependent on the extermination of millions of people? Are these the words of an insane man? Raul
Hilberg gives us the best answer to a question which my students unfailingly
ask every semester: 'You have all heard the saying that a bureaucrat is merely
a cog in the wheel – it turns whenever the wheel is turning. As a political
scientist, I have a different view: the bureaucrat drives the wheel – without
him, it would not turn. And who were these drivers? They were, by and large,
like the men in the railroads, trained representatives of a society, rather than
its aberrants, deviants or outcasts.'[9]

In conclusion, we listen to Walter Stier, former head of the Reich Railway
Department 33 as he is interviewed by Claude Lanzmann for the film *Shoah*.
When asked, if he knew that Treblinka meant extermination, he responds:

> Of course not . . . How could we know? I never went to Treblinka.
> I stayed in Krakow, in Warsaw, glued to my desk . . . I was strictly
> a bureaucrat![10]

Stier condemns himself and the entire Nazi bureaucrat system, for to be a
bureaucrat meant following orders with unquestioning loyalty and very likely

included the task of writing a memorandum like the one we've studied, with its horrifying and yet all too common euphemisms of death.

Notes

1 Claude Lanzmann, *Shoah – An Oral History of the Holocaust* (New York: Pantheon Books, 1985), 103–105.
2 Ibid., 139.
3 Ibid., 103.
4 Alan Rosenberg, 'An Assault on Western values', in *Dimensions*, Vol. I, No. I (Spring 1985), 8.
5 Christopher R. Browning, *Fateful Months. Essays on the Emergence of the Final Solution* (New York: Holmes & Meier, 1985), 61.
6 What was supposed to be an emotionally less trying operation, however, turned out to be as devastating an experience for the SS as open pit killings. The troops who disposed of the bodies in the moveable vans of Russia found horribly distorted faces and bodies covered with vomit and excrement. This was caused by the use of an impure exhaust gas as well as the fact that the vans were driven over rough terrain while gas was being filtered into the compartment. It was only later at Chelmno concentration camp that the chemicals were perfected and the vans remained stationary during the gassing operations. See Browning, op. cit., 64.
7 Raul Hilberg, *Documents of Destruction* (Chicago: Quadrangle Books, 1971), 88.
8 Hannah Arendt, *Eichmann in Jerusalem: A Report on the Banality of Evil* (New York: The Viking Press, 1963), 122.
9 Raul Hilberg, 'The Significance of the Holocaust', in Henry Friedlander and Sybil Milton (eds), *The Holocaust: Ideology, Bureaucracy and Genocide*, (New York: Krauss International Publications, 1980), 99.
10 Lanzmann, op. cit., 135.

Source: Richard Kalfus (unpublished – materials located in curricular section at Yad Vashem, Jerusalem, ref: A-29.3)

Yossel Rakover's appeal to God (an excerpt) 7

A literary reconstruction of a pious Jew's last thoughts by Zvi Kolitz

In the ruins of the Ghetto of Warsaw, among heaps of charred rubbish, there was found, packed tightly into a small bottle, the following testament, written during the ghetto's last hours by a Jew named Yossel Rakover.

WARSAW, April 28, 1943

I, Yossel, son of David Rakover of Tarnopol, a Chasid of the rabbi of Ger and a descendant of the great and pious families of Rakover and Meisel, inscribe these lines as the houses of the Warsaw Ghetto go up in flames. The house I am in is one of the last unburnt houses remaining. For several hours an unusually heavy artillery barrage has been crashing down on us, and the walls are disintegrating under the fire. It will not be long before the house I am in is transformed, like almost every other house of the ghetto, into a grave for its defenders . . .

In a forest where I once hid, I encountered a dog one night, sick and hungry, his tail between his legs. Both of us immediately felt the kinship of our situation. He cuddled up to me, buried his head in my lap, and licked my hands. I do not know if I ever cried so much as that night. I threw my arms around his neck, crying like a baby. If I say that I envied the animals at that moment, it would not be remarkable. But what I felt was more than envy. It was shame. I felt ashamed before the dog to be a man. That is how matters stand. That is the spiritual level to which we have sunk. Life is a tragedy, death a saviour; man a calamity, the beast an ideal; the day a horror, the night – relief.

When my wife, my children and I – six in all – hid in the forest, it was the night and the night alone that concealed us in its bosom. The day turned us over to our persecutors and murderers. I remember with the most painful clarity the day when the Germans raked with a hail of fire the thousands of refugees on the highway from Grodno to Warsaw. As the sun rose, the airplanes zoomed over us and the whole day long they murdered us. In this massacre my wife, with our seven-months-old child in her arms, perished. Two of my five remaining children also disappeared that day without a trace. Their names were David and Yehuda, one was four years old, the other six.

At sunset the handful of survivors continued their journey in the direction of Warsaw, and I, with my three remaining children, started out to comb the fields and woods at the site of the massacre in search of the children. The entire night we called for them, but only echoes replied. I never saw my two children again, and, later, in a dream, I was told that they were in God's hands.

My other three children died in the space of a single year in the Warsaw Ghetto. Rachel, my daughter of ten, heard that it was possible to find scraps of bread in the public dump outside the ghetto walls. The ghetto was starving at the time, and the people who died of starvation lay in the streets like heaps of rags. The people of the ghetto were prepared to face any death but the death of hunger. Against no death did they struggle so fiercely as against death by starvation.

My daughter, Rachel, told me nothing of her plan to steal out of the ghetto, which was punishable by death. She and a girl friend of the same age started out on the perilous journey. She left home under cover of darkness, and at sunrise she and her friend were caught outside the ghetto walls. Nazi ghetto guards, together with dozens of their Polish underlings, at once started in pursuit of those two Jewish children who dared to venture out to hunt for a piece of bread in a garbage can. People witnessing the chase could not believe their eyes. It was unusual even in the ghetto. It looked like a pursuit of dangerous criminals . . . my child, running with her last ounce of strength, fell exhausted to the ground and the Nazis put a bullet through her head. The other child saved herself, but, driven out of her mind, died two weeks later.

The fifth child, Yacob, a boy of thirteen, died on his Bar Mitzvah day of tuberculosis. The last child, my fifteen-year-old daughter, Chaya, perished during a Kinderaktion – a children's operation – that began at sunrise late Rosh Hashanah [Jewish New Year] and ended at sundown. That day, before sunset, hundreds of Jewish families lost their children.

Now my time has come. And like Job, I can say to myself, nor am I the only one who can say it, that I return to the soil naked, as naked as the day of my birth.

I am forty-three years old, and when I look back on the past I can assert confidently, as confident as a man can of himself, that I have lived a respectable, upstanding life, my heart full of love for God. I was once blessed with success, but never boasted of it. My possessions were extensive. My house was open to the needy. I served God enthusiastically, and my single request to Him was that He should allow me to worship Him with all my heart, and all my soul, and all my strength.

I cannot say that my relationship to God has remained unchanged after everything I have lived through, but I can say with absolute certainty that my belief in Him has not changed by a hair's breadth. Previously, when I was happy and well off, my relation to God was as to one who granted me a favour for nothing, and I was eternally obliged to Him for it. Now my relations to Him are as to one who owes me something, too, who owes me very much in fact, and since I feel it so, I believe I have the right to demand it of Him. But I do not say like Job that God should point out my sin with His finger so that I may know why I deserve this; for greater and saintlier men than I are now firmly convinced that it is not a question of punishing sinners: something entirely different is taking place in the world. It is, namely, a time when God has veiled His countenance from the world, sacrificing mankind to its wild instincts. This, however, does not mean that the pious members of my people should justify the edict, saying that God and His judgments are correct. For to say that we deserve the blows we have received is to malign ourselves, to desecrate the Holy Name of God's children. And those who desecrate our name desecrate the Name of the Lord; God is maligned by our self-deprecation.

In a situation like this I naturally expect no miracles, nor do I ask Him, my Lord, to show me mercy. May he treat me with the same indifference with which He treated millions of His people. I am no exception, and I expect no special treatment. I will no longer attempt to save myself, nor flee any more. I will facilitate the work of the fire by moistening my clothing with gasoline. I have three bottles of gasoline left after having emptied several scores over the heads of the murderers. It was one of the finest moments of my life when I did this, and I was shaken with laughter by it. I never dreamed that the death of people, even of enemies – even such enemies – could cause me such great pleasure . . .

I have three more bottles of gasoline. They are as precious to me as wine to a drunkard. After pouring one over my clothes, I will place the paper on which I write these lines in the empty bottle and hide it among the bricks filling the window of this room. If anyone ever finds it and reads it, he will perhaps, understand the emotions of a Jew, one of millions, who died forsaken by the God in Whom he believed unshakeably. I will let the two other bottles explode on the heads of the murderers when my last moment comes.

There were twelve of us using this room at the outbreak of the rebellion. For nine days we battled against the enemy. All eleven of my comrades had fallen, dying silently in battle, including the small boy of about five – who came here only God knows how and who now lies dead near me, with his face wearing the kind of smile that appears on children's faces when dreaming peacefully – even this child died with the same epic calm as his older comrades . . .

Unless my face is eaten by the flames, a similar smile may rest on it after my death. Meanwhile, I still live, and before my death I wish to speak to my Lord as a living man, a simple, living person who had the great but tragic honour of being a Jew.

I am proud that I am a Jew not in spite of the world's treatment of us, but precisely because of this treatment. I should be ashamed to belong to the people who spawned and raised the criminals who are responsible for the deeds that have been perpetrated against us or to any people who tolerated these deeds.

I am proud to be a Jew because it is an art to be a Jew. It is no art to be an Englishman, an American or a Frenchman. It may be easier, more comfortable to be one of them, but not more honourable. Yes, it is an honour, a terrible honour to be a Jew!

I believe that to be a Jew means to be a fighter, an everlasting swimmer against the turbulent human current. The Jew is a hero, a martyr, a saint. You, our evil enemies, declare that we are bad. I believe that we are better and finer than you, but even if we were worse, I should like to see how you would look in our place!

I am happy to belong to the unhappiest of all peoples of the world, whose precepts represent the loftiest and most beautiful of all morality and laws. These immortal precepts which we possess have now been even more sanctified and immortalized by the fact that they have been so debased and insulted by the enemies of the Lord.

I believe that to be a Jew is an inborn trait. One is born a Jew exactly as one is born an artist. It is impossible to be released from being a Jew. That is our godly attribute that has made us a chosen people. Those who do not understand this will never understand the higher meaning of our martyrdom. If ever I doubted that God once designated us as the chosen people, I would believe now that our tribulations have made us the chosen one.

I believe in You, God of Israel, even though You have done everything to stop me from believing in You. I believe in Your laws even if I cannot excuse Your actions. My relationship to You is not the relationship of a slave to his master but rather that of a pupil to his teacher. I bow my head before Your greatness, but I will not kiss the lash with which You strike me.

You say, I know, that we have sinned, O Lord. It must surely be true! And therefore we are punished? I can understand that too! But I should like You to tell me whether *there is any sin in the world deserving of such a punishment as the punishment we have received.*

You assert that You will yet repay our enemies? I am convinced of it! Repay them without mercy? I have no doubt about that either! I should like You to tell me, however – *is there any punishment in the world capable of compensating for crimes that have been committed against us?*

You say, I know, that it is no longer a question of sin and punishment, but rather a situation in which Your countenance is veiled, in which humanity is abandoned to its evil instincts. But I should like to ask You, O Lord – and this question burns in me like a consuming fire – *what more, O, what more must transpire before You unveil Your countenance again to the world?*

I want to say to You that now, more than in any previous period in eternal path of agony, we, we the tortured, the humiliated, the buried alive and burned alive, we the insulted, the mocked, the lonely, the forsaken by God and man – we have the right to know *what are the limits of Your forbearance?*

I should like to say something more: do not put the rope under too much strain, lest, alas, it snaps! The test to which You have put us is so severe, so unbearably severe, that You should – You must – forgive those members of Your people who, in their misery, have turned from You.

Forgive those who have turned from You in their misery, but also those who have turned from You in their happiness. You have transformed our life into such a frightful, perpetual ordeal that the cowards among us have been forced to flee from it; and what is happiness but a place of refuge for cowards? Do not chastise them for it. One does not strike cowards, but has mercy on them. Have mercy on *them*, rather than *us*, O Lord.

Forgive those who have desecrated Your name, who have gone over to the service of other gods, who have become indifferent to You. You have castigated them so severely that they no longer believe that You are their Father, that they have any Father at all.

I tell You this because I do believe in You, because I believe in You more strongly than ever, because now I know that You are my Lord because after all You are not, You cannot possibly be after all the God of those whose deeds are the most horrible expression of ungodliness!

If You are not *my* Lord, then whose Lord are You? The Lord of the murderers?

If those that hate me and murder me are so benighted, so evil, what then am I if not he who reflects something of Your light, of Your goodness?

I cannot extol You for the deeds that You tolerate. I bless You and extol You, however, for the very fact of Your existence, for Your awesome mightiness!

The murderers themselves have already passed sentence on themselves and will never escape it, but may You carry out a doubly severe sentence on those who are condoning the murder.

Those who condemn murder orally, but rejoice at in their hearts . . . Those who meditate in their foul hearts: it is fitting, after all to say that he is evil, the tyrant, but he carries out a bit of work for us for which we will always be grateful to him!

It is written in Your Torah that a thief should be punished more severely than a brigand, in spite of the fact that the thief does not attack his victim physically and merely attempts to take his possessions stealthily.

The reason for this is that a robber by attacking his victim in broad daylight shows no more fear of man than of God. The thief, on the other hand, fears man, but not God. His punishment, therefore, is greater.

I should be satisfied if You dealt with the murderers as with brigands, for their attitude towards You and towards us is the same.

But those who are silent in the face of murder, those who have no fears of You but fear what people might say . . . those who express their sympathy with the drowning man but refuse to rescue him though they can swim – punish them, O Lord, punish them, I implore with a doubly severe sentence!

Death can wait no longer. From the floors above me, the firing becomes weaker by the minute. The last defenders of this stronghold are now falling, and with them falls and perishes the great, beautiful, and God-fearing Jewish part of Warsaw. The sun is about to set, and I thank God that I will never see it again. Fire lights my small window, and the bit of sky that I can see is flooded with red like a waterfall of blood. In about an hour at the most I will be with the rest of my family and with the millions of other stricken members of my people in that better world where there are no more questions.

I die peacefully, but not complacently; persecuted, but not enslaved; embittered, but not cynical; a believer, but not a supplicant; a lover of God, but no blind amen-sayer of His.

I have followed Him even when He rejected me. I have followed His commandments even when He castigated me for it; I have loved Him and I love Him even when He hurls me to the earth, tortures me to death, makes me an object of shame and ridicule.

My rabbi would frequently tell the story of a Jew who fled from the Spanish Inquisition with his wife and child, striking out in a small boat over the stormy sea until he reached a rocky island where a flash of lightning killed his wife; a storm rose and hurled his son into the sea. Then, as lonely as a stone, naked, barefoot, lashed by the storm and terrified by the thunder and the lightning, hands turned up to God, the Jew, setting out on his journey through the wastes of the island, turned to his maker with the following words:

'God of Israel, I have fled to this place in order to worship You without molestation, to obey Your commandments and sanctify Your name. You, however, have done everything to make me stop believing in You. Now lest it seem to You that You will succeed by these tribulations to drive me from the right path, I notify

You, my God and the God of my fathers, *that it will not avail You in the least!* You may insult me, You may castigate me, You may take from me all that I cherish and hold dear in the world, You may torture me to death – I shall believe in *You,* I shall love You no matter what You do to test me.'

And these are my last words to You, my wrathful God: nothing will avail You in the least. You have done everything to make me renounce You, to make me lose my faith in You, but I die exactly as I have lived, a *believer!*

Eternally praised be the God of the dead, the God of vengeance, of truth and of law, Who will soon show His face to the world again and shake its foundations with His almighty voice.

Hear, O Israel, the lord our God the Lord is One.

Into your hands, O Lord, I consign my soul.

Source: Zvi Kolitz in Albert Friedlander (ed.), Out of the Whirlwind: A Reader of Holocaust Literature *(Schocken Books, 1976)*

Note: This 'document' is, in fact, a work of literary reconstruction, although there *was* a Chasidic family called Rakover which perished during the Holocaust. Here the author, Zvi Kolitz, recreates the last thoughts of a pious Jew.

The power of indifference 8

The following poem, together with the questions which follow it, addresses one of the major themes that a study of the Holocaust embraces: the consequences of standing idly by while others are in distress: that to turn away from an injustice is to compound it; that those who witness wrong-doing share in the responsibility for its occurrence; and that everyone can make a difference. For indifference, far from being innocent and innocuous, is a definite choice that we make and an active player on the stage of human history. Or as Ian Kershaw has written, with respect to the Nazi period,

> Popular opinion, largely indifferent and infused with a latent anti-Jewish feeling, further bolstered by propaganda, provided the climate within which the spiralling Nazi aggression towards the Jews could take place unchallenged . . .
>
> The road to Auschwitz was built by hate but paved with indifference.

The Hangman

1.

Into our town the Hangman came,
Smelling of gold and blood and flame –
And he paced our bricks with a diffident air
And built his frame on the courthouse square.

The scaffold stood by the courthouse side.
Only as wide as the door was wide;
A frame as tall, or little more,
Than the capping sill of the courthouse door.

And we wondered, whenever we had the time,
Who the criminal, what the crime,
That Hangman judged with the yellow twist
Of knotted hemp in his busy fist.

And innocent though we were, with dread
We passed those eyes of buckshot lead;
Till one cried: 'Hangman, who is he
For whom you raise the gallows-tree?'

Then a twinkle grew in the buckshot eye,
And he gave us a riddle instead of reply:
'He who serves me best,' said he,
'Shall earn the rope on the gallows-tree.'

And he stepped down, and laid his hand
On a man who came from another land.
And we breathed again, for another's grief
At the Hangman's hand was our relief.

And the gallows-frame on the courthouse lawn
By tomorrow's sun would be struck and gone.
So we gave him way, and no one spoke,
Out of respect for his hangman's cloak.

2.

The next day's sun looked mildly down
On roof and street in our quiet town
And, stark and black in the morning air,
The gallows-tree on the courthouse square.

And the Hangman stood at his usual stand
With the yellow hemp in his busy hand;
With his buckshot eye and his jaw like a pike
And his air so knowing and businesslike.

And we cried: 'Hangman, have you not done,
Yesterday, with the alien one?'
Then we fell silent, and stood amazed:
'Oh, not for him was the gallows raised . . . '

He laughed a laugh as he looked at us:
' . . . Did you think I'd gone to all this fuss
To hang one man? That's a thing I do
To stretch the rope when the rope is new.'

Then one cried 'Murderer!' One cried 'Shame!'
And into our midst the Hangman came
To that man's place. 'Do you hold,' said he,
'With him that's meant for the gallows-tree?'

And he laid his hand on that one's arm,
And we shrank back in quick alarm,
And we gave him way, and no one spoke
Out of fear of his hangman's cloak.

That night we saw with dread surprise
The Hangman's scaffold had grown in size.
Fed by the blood beneath the chute
The gallows-tree had taken root;

Now as wide, or a little more,
Than the steps that led to the courthouse door,
As tall as the writing, or nearly as tall,
Halfway up on the courthouse wall.

3.

The third he took – and we had all heard tell –
Was a usurer and infidel. And:
'What,' said the Hangman, 'have you to do
With the gallows-bound, and he a Jew?'

And we cried out: 'Is this one he
Who has served you well and faithfully?'
The Hangman smiled: 'It's a clever scheme
To try the strength of the gallows-beam.'

The fourth man's dark, accusing song
Had scratched out comfort, hard and long:
And 'What concern,' he gave us back,
Have you for the doomed – the doomed and black?'

The fifth. The sixth. And we cried again:
'Hangman, Hangman, is this the man?'

'It's a trick,' he said, 'that we hangmen know
For easing the trap when the trap springs slow.'

And so we ceased and asked no more,
As the Hangman tallied his bloody score:
And sun by sun, and night by night,
The gallows grew to monstrous height.

The wings of the scaffold opened wide
Till they covered the square from side to side;
And the monster cross-beam, looking down,
Cast its shadow across the town.

4.

Then through the town the Hangman came
And called in the empty streets my name
And I looked at the gallows soaring tall
And thought: 'There is no one left at all
For hanging, and so he calls to me
To help him pull down the gallows-tree.'
And I went out with right good hope
To the Hangman's tree and the Hangman's rope.

He smiled at me as I came down
To the courthouse square through the silent town,
And supple and stretched in his busy hand
Was the yellow twist of the hempen strand.

And he whistled his tune as he tried the trap
And it sprang down with a ready snap –
And then with a smile of awful command
He laid his hand upon my hand.

'You tricked me, Hangman!' I shouted then,
'That your scaffold was built for other men . . .
And I no henchman of yours,' I cried.
'You lied to me, Hangman, foully lied!'

Then a twinkle grew in the buckshot eye:
'Lied to you? Tricked you?' he said, 'Not I
For I answered you straight and I told you true:
The scaffold was raised for none but you.

'For who has served me more faithfully
Than you with your coward's hope?' said he,
'And where are the others that might have stood
Side by your side in the common good?'

'Dead,' I whispered: and amiably,
'Murdered,' the Hangman corrected me;
'First the alien, then the Jew . . .
I did no more than you let me do.'

Beneath the beam that blocked the sky,
None had stood so alone as I –
And the Hangman strapped me, and no voice there
Cried 'Stay' for me in the empty square.

Maurice Ogden

Discussion Questions

1 What choices were open to the people in the town when the Hangman arrived?
2 What choices were open to them by the time he had finished his work in the town?
3 Was there a way to stop the Hangman? If so, how? If not, why not?
4 How does the poem relate to Germany in the 1930s? To society today?
5 In 1933 Martin Niemöller, a leader of the Confessing Church, voted for the Nazi Party. By 1938, he was in a concentration camp. After the war, he is believed to have said, 'In Germany, the Nazis came for the Communists, and I didn't speak up because I wasn't a Communist. Then they came for the Jews, and I didn't speak up because I wasn't a Jew. Then they came for the trade unionists, and I didn't speak up because I wasn't a trade unionist. Then they came for the Catholics, and I didn't speak up because I was a Protestant, Then they came for me, and by that time there was no one left to speak for me.' How is the point Niemöller makes similar to the one Maurice Ogden makes in 'The Hangman'?
6 What is the meaning of the Hangman's riddle: 'He who serves me best,' said he, 'shall earn the rope on the gallows-tree'?

Source: Facing History and Ourselves – Resource Book *(Facing History and Ourselves Inc., 1994), p. 206*

PART II

SELECTED KEY DOCUMENTS

The Nazi Party's intense hostility towards communists and Jews was matched by the warmth of its embrace of the ordinary German: for every Jewish vice, so its propaganda went, there was a stout, respectable German virtue. This appeal to middle-class values is very evident in the following 'upright' piece which was widely disseminated by the Nazis. Only the last verse betrays that it was not a product of the Nazi era; it was, in fact, written by one of their most revered mentors, Theodor Fritsch, the late nineteenth-century antisemitic politician:

1. Be proud of being a German and strive earnestly and steadily to practise the inherited virtues of our people – courage, faithfulness and veracity – and to inspire and develop these in your children.

2. Thou shalt know that thou, together with all thy fellow Germans, regardless of faith or creed, hast a common implacable foe. His name is Jew.

3. Thou shalt keep thy blood pure. Consider it a crime to soil the noble Aryan breed of thy people by mingling it with the Jewish breed. For thou must know that Jewish blood is everlasting, putting the Jewish stamp on body and soul unto the farthest generations.

4. Thou shalt be helpful to thou fellow German and further him in all matters not counter to the German conscience, the more so if he be pressed by the Jew. Thou shalt at once take into court any offence or crime committed by the Jew in deed, word or letter, that comes to thy knowledge, lest the Jew abuse the laws of our country with impunity.

5. Thou shalt have no social intercourse with the Jew. Avoid all contact and community with the Jew and keep him away from thyself and thy family, especially thy daughters, lest they suffer injury of body and soul.

6. Thou shalt have no business relations with the Jews. Never choose a Jew as a business partner, nor borrow nor buy from him, and keep your wife, too, from doing so. Thou shalt sell nothing to him, nor use him as an agent in thy transactions, that thou mayest remain free and not become slave unto the Jew nor help increase his money, which is the power by which he enslaves our people.

7. Thou shalt drive the Jew from thy own breast and take no example from Jewish tricks and Jewish wiles, for thou shalt never match the Jew in trickery but forfeit thy honour and earn the contempt of thy fellow Germans and the punishment of the courts.

8. Thou shalt not entrust thy rights to a Jewish lawyer, nor thy children to a Jewish physician, nor thy children to a Jewish teacher lest thy honour, body and soul suffer harm.

9. Thou shalt not lend ear nor give credence to the Jew. Keep away all Jewish writings from thy German home and hearth lest their lingering poison may unnerve and corrupt thyself and thy family.

10. Thou shalt use no violence against the Jews because it is unworthy of thee and against the law. But if a Jew attacks thee, ward off his Semitic insolence with German wrath.

Source: Theodor Fritsch, The Antisemitic Catechism *(1883), later renamed* Handbook on the Jewish Question. *The English version is cited in Paul Massing,* Rehearsal for Destruction: A Study of Political Antisemitism in Imperial Germany *(Harper and Row, 1949)*

2 The *Protocols of the Elders of Zion*

A favourite antisemitic image from the late nineteenth century was that of the power-crazed Jews engaged in an international conspiracy to undermine the safe and peaceful world of the gentiles, fomenting wars, revolutions, dangerous ideologies and the collapse of organized religion.

The *Protocols of the Elders of Zion* is the single most notorious antisemitic publication of this type – and certainly the most damaging in its long-term effects. A literary hoax hatched in all probability by an agent of the Russian secret police – in imitation of a French satire, itself entirely unconnected with Jews – it painted a startling picture of an international Jewish leadership bent on world domination and using all the forces of the modern world to achieve it. (The sinister term 'elders of Zion' was presumably inspired by the First Zionist Congress which was held in 1897, around the time the *Protocols* were concocted.)

Though it had little impact in Russia itself, after being brought to the west by White Russians fleeing the Bolshevik Revolution it was translated into several different languages and enjoyed wide circulation between the wars, especially in Weimar and later Nazi Germany. (It is still available in many countries today!) The following is a brief, but representative extract:

Protocol Number I

. . . Political Freedom is not a fact but an idea. One must know how to employ this idea when it becomes necessary to attract popular forces to one's party by mental allurement if it plans to crush the party in power. The task is made easier if the opponent himself has contradicted the idea of freedom, embracing liberalism, and thereby yielding his power. It is precisely here that the triumph of our theory becomes apparent; the relinquished reins of power are, according to the laws of nature, immediately seized by a new hand because the blind force of the people cannot remain without a leader even for one day, and the new power merely replaces the old, weakened by liberalism.

In our day the power of *gold* has replaced liberal rulers. There was a time when faith ruled. The idea of freedom cannot be realised because no one knows how to make reasonable use of it. Give the people self-government for a short time and it will become corrupted. From that very moment strife begins and soon develops into social struggle, as a result of which states are set aflame and their authority is reduced to ashes.

Whether the state is exhausted by internal convulsions, or whether civil wars deliver it into the hands of external enemies, in either case it can be regarded as hopelessly lost: it is in our power. The despotism of capital, which is entirely in our hands, holds out to it a straw which the state must grasp, although against its will, or otherwise fall into the abyss . . .

Our motto is Power and Hypocrisy. Only power can conquer in politics, especially if it is concealed in talents which are necessary to statesmen. Violence must be the principle; hypocrisy and cunning the rule of those governments which do not wish to lay down their crowns at the feet of the agents of some new power. This evil is the sole means of attaining the good. For this reason we must not hesitate at bribery, fraud, and treason when these can help us to reach our end. In politics it is necessary to seize the property of others without hesitation if in so doing we attain submission and power . . .

In all parts of the world the words, *Liberty, Equality and Fraternity* have brought whole legions into our ranks through our . . . agents, carrying the banner with delight. Meanwhile these words were worms which ruined the prosperity of the *Goys*, everywhere destroying peace, quiet and solidarity, undermining all the foundations of their states. You will see subsequently that this aided our triumph, for it also gave us, among other things, the opportunity to grasp the trump card, the abolition of privileges; in other words, the very essence of the aristocracy of the *Goys*, which was the only protection of peoples and countries against us.

On the ruins of the natural and hereditary aristocracy we have established this new aristocracy on the qualification of wealth, which is dependent upon us, and also upon science which is promoted by our wise men . . .

Protocol Number 2

It is necessary for us that wars, whenever possible, should bring no territorial advantage; this will shift war to an economic basis and force nations to realize the strength of our predominance; such a situation will put both sides at the mercy of our million-eyed international agency, which will be unhampered by any frontiers. Then our international rights will do away with national rights, in a limited sense, and will rule the peoples in the same way as the civil power of each state regulates the relations of its subjects among themselves . . .

Do not think our assertions are without foundation: note the successes of Darwinism, Marxism, and Nietzcheism, engineered by us. The demoralising effects of these doctrines upon the minds of the *Goys* should be already obvious to us . . .

There is one great force in the hands of modern states which arouses thought movements among the people. That is the press. The role of the press is to indicate necessary demands, to register complaints of the people, and to express and foment dissatisfaction. The triumph of free babbling is incarnated in the press; but governments were unable to profit by this power and it has fallen into our hands. Through it we have attained influence, while remaining in the background. Thanks to the press, we have gathered gold in our hands, although we had to take it from rivers of blood and tears.

But it cost us the sacrifice of many of our own people. Every sacrifice on our part is worth a thousand *Goys* before God.

Protocol Number 3

To induce the lovers of authority to abuse their power, we have placed all the forces in opposition to each other, having developed their liberal tendencies towards independence. We have excited different forms of initiative in that direction; we have armed all the parties; we have made authority the target of all ambitions. We have opened the arenas in different states, where revolts are now occurring and disorders and bankruptcy will shortly appear everywhere . . .

Daring journalists, impudent pamphleteers, make daily attacks on the administrative personnel. The abuse of power is definitely preparing the downfall of all institutions and everything will be overturned by the blows of the infuriated mobs . . .

Under our guidance, the people have exterminated aristocracy, which was their natural protector and guardian, for its own interests and inseparably connected with the well-being of the people. Now, however, with the destruction of this aristocracy the masses have fallen under the power of the profiteers and cunning upstarts who have settled on the workers as a merciless burden.

We will present ourselves in the guise of saviours of the workers from this oppression when we suggest that they enter our army of Socialists, Anarchists, Communists, to whom we always extend our help, under the guise of the rule of brotherhood demanded by the human solidarity of our social masonry. The aristocracy which benefited by the labour of the people by right was interested that the workers should be well fed, healthy and strong.

We, on the contrary, are concerned in the opposite – in the degeneration of the *Goys*. Our power lies in the chronic malnutrition and in the weakness of the worker, because through this he falls under our power and is unable to find either strength or energy to combat it.

Hunger gives to capital greater power over the worker than the legal authority of the sovereign ever gave to the aristocracy. Through misery and the resulting jealous hatred we manipulate the mob and crush those who stand in our way . . . This hatred will be still more accentuated by the economic crisis which will stop financial transactions and all industrial life. Having organised a general economic crisis by all possible underhand means, and with the help of gold which is all in our hands, we will throw great crowds of workmen into the street, simultaneously, in all countries of Europe. These crowds will gladly shed the blood of those of whom they, in the simplicity of their ignorance, have been jealous since childhood and whose property they will then be able to loot.

They will not harm our people because we will know of the time of the attack and we will take measures to protect them . . .

Remember the French Revolution, which we have called 'great'; the secrets of its preparation are well known to us, for it was the work of our hands. Since then we have carried the masses from one disappointment to another, so that they will renounce even us in favour of a despot sovereign of Zionist blood, whom we are preparing for the world.

The Balfour Declaration (2 November 1917) 3

At the height of the First World War, as British troops in the Middle East were poised for the capture of Palestine from the Ottoman Turks, the British government made a remarkable undertaking – later to prove highly controversial – to assist in the establishment of a Jewish home in Palestine (the site of biblical Israel). This declaration, which was in effect a statement of intent to the entire Jewish world, took the form of a letter written by the British Foreign Secretary Arthur Balfour and addressed to Lord Lionel Rothschild, Honorary President of the Zionist Federation of Great Britain. Balfour asked Rothschild to communicate its contents to the Zionist Federation. The letter is dated 2 November 1917.

This declaration would later form the basis of the creation of the British Mandate in Palestine (1920–48) and for the eventual establishment of the

State of Israel in 1948. The text of the declaration, taken from the letter, is as follows:

His Majesty's Government view with favour the establishment in Palestine of a national home for the Jewish people and will use their best endeavours to facilitate the achievement of this object, it being clearly understood that nothing shall be done that may prejudice the civil and religious rights of existing non-Jewish communities in Palestine or the rights and political status enjoyed by Jews in other countries.

[Arthur James Balfour, British Foreign Secretary]

4 Adolf Hitler: A Letter on the Jewish Question

This is the earliest recorded expression of Hitler's views on any subject. While it may appear significant that this letter is preoccupied with the Jewish question, it should be borne in mind that it was written expressly in response to a request by Adolf Gemlich, his military superior, who wished to know the place of the Jewish question within the German army's anti-revolutionary propaganda (Hitler was at that time employed as a secret agent of the Press and Propaganda Office of the political department of the *Wehrmacht*).

Precisely what Hitler meant at this early stage (1919) by the words, 'complete removal of the Jews' is impossible to state with certainty. The German he used – *die Entfernung der Juden überhaupt* – is no more specific than its English equivalent. What is clear, however, is his prophetic commitment to a two-staged assault on the Jews of Germany, starting with a systematic 'legal' campaign.

Antisemitism as a political movement should not and cannot be determined by emotional factors, but rather by a realisation of the facts. And these facts are:

First, Jewry is clearly a racial and not a religious group ... All that which is for men a source of higher life – be it religion, socialism or democracy – is for the Jew merely a means to an end, namely, the satisfaction of his lust for power and money.

His actions will result in a racial tuberculosis of peoples.

Hence it follows: antisemitism based on purely emotional grounds will find its ultimate expression in the form of pogroms (which are capricious and thus not truly effective). Rational antisemitism, however, must pursue a systematic, *legal* campaign against the Jews, by the revocation of the special privileges they enjoy in contrast to the other foreigners living among us. But the final objective must be the complete removal of the Jews.

Source: *Adolf Hitler to Adolf Gemlich, 16 September 1919, Haupstaatsarchiv München, in Paul Mendes-Flohr and Jehuda Reinharz (eds)*, The Jew in the Modern World *(Oxford University Press, 1980), p. 484*

The 25-point programme of the National-Socialist German Workers' Party **5**

The following document is the first complete and coherent statement of aims and objectives of the infant Nazi Party. This programme would later form an important part of the basis of the Party's successful appeal to the German electorate.

The Programme of the German Workers' Party is a programme for our time. The leadership rejects the establishment of new aims after those set out in the programme have been achieved, for the sole purpose of making it possible for the Party to continue to exist as the result of the artificially stimulated dissatisfaction of the masses.

1. We demand the uniting of all Germans within one Greater Germany, on the basis of the right to self-determination of nations.

2. We demand equal rights for the German people with respect to other nations, and the annulment of the peace treaty of Versailles and St. Germain.

3. We demand land and soil to feed our People and settle our excess population.

4. Only Nationals can be Citizens of the State. Only persons of German blood can be Nationals, regardless of religious affiliation. No Jew can therefore be a German National.

5. Any person who is not a Citizen will be able to live in Germany only as a guest and must be subject to legislation for Aliens.

6. Only a Citizen is entitled to decide the leadership and laws of the State. We therefore demand that only Citizens may hold public office, regardless of whether it is a national, state or local office.

We oppose the corrupting parliamentary custom of making party considerations, and not character and ability, the criterion for appointments to official positions.

7. We demand that the State make it its duty to provide opportunities of employment first of all for its own Citizens. If it is not possible to maintain the entire

population of the State, then foreign nationals (non-citizens) are to be expelled from the Reich.

8. Any further immigration of non-Germans is to be prevented. We demand that all non-Germans who entered Germany after August 2 1914, be forced to leave the Reich without delay.

9. All German citizens must have equal rights and duties.

10. It must be the first duty of every Citizen to carry out intellectual or physical work. Individual activity must not be harmful to the public interest and must be pursued within the framework of the community and for the general good.

We therefore demand:

11. The abolition of all income obtained without labour or effort.

Breaking the servitude of interest

12. In view of the tremendous sacrifices in property and blood demanded of the Nation by every war, personal gain from the war must be termed a crime against the Nation. We therefore demand the total confiscation of all war profits.

13. We demand the nationalization of all enterprises (already) converted into corporations (trusts).

14. We demand profit-sharing in large enterprises.

15. We demand the large-scale development of age-old pension schemes.

16. We demand the creation and maintenance of a sound middle class; the immediate communalization of the large department stores, which are to be leased at low rates to small tradesmen. We demand the most careful consideration for the owners of small businesses in orders placed by national, state or community authorities.

17. We demand land reform in accordance with our national needs and a law for expropriation without compensation of land for public purposes. Abolition of ground rent and prevention of all speculation in land.

18. We demand ruthless battle against those who harm the common good by their activities. Persons committing base crimes against the People, usurers, profiteers, etc., are to be punished by death without regard to religion or race.

19. We demand the replacement of Roman Law, which serves a materialistic World Order, by German Law.

20. In order to make higher education – and thereby entry into leading positions – available to every able and industrious German, the State must provide a thorough restructuring of our entire public educational system. The courses of study at all

educational institutions are to be adjusted to meet the requirements of practical life. Understanding of the concept of the State must be achieved through the schools (teaching of civics) at the earliest age at which it can be grasped. We demand the education at the public expense of specially gifted children of poor parents, without regard to the latters' position or occupation.

21. The State must raise the level of national health by means of mother-and-child care, the banning of juvenile labour, achievement of physical fitness through legislation for compulsory gymnastics and sports, and maximum support for all organizations providing physical training for young people.

22. We demand the abolition of hireling troops and the creation of a national army.

23. We demand laws to fight against *deliberate* political lies and their dissemination by the press. In order to make it possible to create a German press, we demand:
  (a) all editors and editorial employees of newspapers appearing in the German language must be German by race;
  (b) non-German newspapers require express permission from the State for their publication. They may not be printed in the German language;
  (c) any financial participation in a German newspaper or influence on such a paper is to be forbidden by law to non-Germans and the penalty for any breach of this law will be the closing of the newspaper in question, as well as the immediate expulsion from the Reich of the non-Germans involved.

Newspapers which violate the public interest are to be banned. We demand laws against trends in art and literature which have a destructive effect on our national life, and the suppression of performances that offend against the above requirements.

24. We demand freedom for all religious denominations, provided they do not endanger the existence of the State or offend the concepts of decency and morality of the Germanic race. The Party as such stands for positive Christianity, without associating itself with any particular denomination. It fights against the Jewish-materialistic spirit *within* and around us, and is convinced that a permanent revival of our Nation can be achieved only from *within*, on the basis of:

Public interest before private interest

25. To carry out all the above we demand: the creation of a strong central authority in the Reich. Unquestioned authority by the political central Parliament over the entire Reich and over its organizations in general. The establishment of trade and professional organizations to enforce the Reich basic laws in the individual states.

The Party leadership promises to take an uncompromising stand, at the cost of their own lives if need be, on the enforcement of the above points.

Munich, February 24, 1920

Source: Das Programm der NSDAP *(Berlin, 1933). Translation appears in Yitzhak Arad, Yisrael Gutman, and Abraham Margaliot (eds),* Documents on the Holocaust: Selected Sources on the Destruction of the Jews of Germany and Austria, Poland, and the Soviet Union *(Yad Vashem Publications, 1981)*

6 The Nuremberg Laws

On 15 September 1935, at its annual Party Congress at Nuremberg, the Nazi Government passed two momentous decrees as part of an overall legal assault upon the Jews of Germany.

The first law stripped all Jews of their citizenship, reversing at a stroke the entire process of Jewish emancipation, which the Jews of Germany had struggled to achieve since the French Revolution of 1789 (emancipation had eventually been granted with the unification of Germany in 1871).

The second law outlawed marriage and sexual relations between Jews and those of 'German or related blood'. An implementing decree of 14 November 1935 defined more precisely the terms 'Jew', 'Aryan' and 'Mischling' (one of mixed parentage). Christians whose parents or grandparents were Jewish could now be considered as full Jews for all purposes. The Nuremberg Laws effectively institutionalized Nazi racism and served as the basis for many further anti-Jewish regulations and pronouncements.

What follows is an excerpt from the two Nuremberg Laws and the Implementing Decree.

Reich Citizenship Laws
15 September, 1935

Paragraph 2

1) A Reich citizen is a subject of the State who is of German or related blood, who proves by his conduct that he is willing and fit faithfully to serve the German people and Reich.

2) Reich citizenship is acquired through the granting of a Reich Citizenship Certificate.

3) The Reich citizen is the sole bearer of full political rights in accordance with the Law.

Law for the Protection of German Blood and Honour
15 September, 1935

Moved by the understanding that purity of the German Blood is the essential condition for the continued existence of the German people, and inspired by the inflexible determination to ensure the existence of the German nation for all time, the Reichstag has unanimously adopted the following Law, which is promulgated herewith:

Paragraph 1

1) Marriages between Jews and subjects of the State of German or related blood are forbidden. Marriages nevertheless concluded are invalid, even if concluded abroad to circumvent this law.

2) Annulment proceedings can be initiated only by the State Prosecutor.

Paragraph 2

Extra-marital sexual relations between Jews and subjects of the State of German or related blood are forbidden.

Paragraph 3

Jews may not employ in their households female subjects of the State of German or related blood who are under 45 years of age.

Paragraph 4

1) Jews are forbidden to fly the Reich or National flag or to display the Reich colours.

2) They are, on the other hand, permitted to display the Jewish colours. The exercise of this right is protected by the State.

Paragraph 5

1) Any person who violates the prohibition under Paragraph 1 will be punished by a prison sentence with hard labour.

2) A male who violates the prohibition under Paragraph 2 will be punished with a prison sentence with or without hard labour.

3) Any person violating the provisions under Paragraphs 3 or 4 will be punished with a prison sentence of up to one year and a fine, or with one or the other of these penalties.

First [Implementing] Decree to the Reich Citizenship Law
14 November, 1935

Paragraph 4

1) A Jew cannot be a Reich citizen. He has no voting rights in political matters; he cannot occupy a public office.

2) Jewish officials will retire as of 31 December, 1935 . . .

Paragraph 5

1) A Jew is a person descended from at least three Jewish grandparents who are full Jews by race.

2) A subject of the State of mixed descent (Mischling) who is descended from two full Jewish grandparents is also considered a Jew if: (a) he belonged to the Jewish religious community at the time this law was issued or joined the community later; (b) he was married to a Jew at the time the law was issued, or if he married a Jew subsequently; (c) he is the offspring of a marriage with a Jew, which was contracted after the Law for the Protection of German Blood and Honour went into effect; or (d) he is the offspring of extra-marital intercourse with a Jew and will be born out of wedlock after 31 July, 1936.

Source: Reichsgesetzblatt, I, *(1935, p. 1333). English translation by Priscilla Fishman in Yisrael Gutman and Chaim Schatzker,* The Holocaust and its Significance *(Zalman Shazar Center, 1984, except for paragraph 5, 2) which appears in Bernard Dov Weinryb,* Jewish Emancipation Under Attack *(The American Jewish Publication Committee, 1942) reproduced in Paul Mendes-Flohr and Jehuda Reinharz (eds),* The Jew in the Modern World *(Oxford University Press, 1980)*

7 An eyewitness response to Kristallnacht

On the night of 9–10 November 1938, in a clearly orchestrated campaign throughout the length and breadth of Germany, gangs of SA thugs, other party members and hooligans roamed the streets in an orgy of violence. The operation took the form of the destruction or burning of synagogues, the

2 Destruction of the synagogues, 9/10 November 1938

ransacking of Jewish shops and warehouses and the terrorization, beating up and murder of Jewish individuals. According to the Nazis' own reports, 91 Jews were killed, more than 7,000 Jewish-owned shops destroyed and approximately 300 synagogues razed to the ground. The Nazis were apparently impressed by all the broken glass from the synagogue windows and named this violent night 'Kristallnacht' (the Night of Shattered Glass).

The reaction abroad was predictably outraged. And even among ordinary Germans, the general response was far from supportive of, and at worst indifferent towards, their own government's measures at that time. From then on, concerted physical attacks against Jews – including, after 1941, mass systematic extermination – would take place outside German soil.

The American consul in Leipzig described the event and the public reaction to it in these words:

The shattering of shop windows, looting of stores and dwellings of Jews ... was hailed subsequently in the Nazi press as a 'spontaneous wave of righteous indignation throughout Germany' ... So far as a high percentage of the German populace is concerned, a state of popular indignation that would lead to such excesses can be considered as non-existent. On the contrary, in viewing the ruins and attendant measures employed, all of the local crowds observed were obviously benumbed over what had happened and aghast over the unprecedented fury of Nazi acts that had been or were taking place with bewildering rapidity . . .

At 3 a.m. on 10 November 1938 was unleashed a barrage of Nazi ferocity as had had no equal hitherto in Germany, or very likely anywhere else in the world since savagery began. Jewish buildings were smashed into and contents demolished or looted. In one of the Jewish sections an eighteen-year-old boy was hurled from a three-storey window to land with both legs broken on a street littered with burning beds and other household furniture and effects from his family's and other apartments . . . It is reported . . . that among domestic effects thrown out of a Jewish building, a small dog descended four flights on to a cluttered street with a broken spine.

Three synagogues in Leipzig were fired simultaneously by incendiary bombs and all sacred objects and records desecrated or destroyed, in most cases hurled through the windows and burned in the streets. No attempts whatsoever were made to quench the fires, the activity of the fire brigade being confined to playing water on adjoining buildings . . .

Tactics which closely approached the ghoulish took place at the Jewish cemetery where the temple was fired together with a building occupied by caretakers, tombstones uprooted and graves violated. Eyewitnesses considered reliable the report that ten corpses were left unburied at this cemetery for a whole week because all gravediggers and cemetery attendants had been arrested . . .

Having demolished dwellings and hurled most of the movable effects onto the streets, the insatiably sadistic perpetrators threw many of the trembling inmates into a small stream that flows through the Zoological Park, commanding horrified spectators to spit at them, defile them with mud and jeer at their plight. The latter incident has been repeatedly corroborated by German witnesses who were nauseated in telling the tale . . . These tactics were carried out the entire morning of 10 November without police intervention and they were applied to men, women and children.

Source: The full report from which this extract is taken appears in Jeremy Noakes and Geoffrey Pridham (eds), Nazism 1919–1945. A Documentary Reader, *Vol. II:* State, Society and Economy *(Exeter University Press, 1984), Document 424*

German Foreign Ministry 8
memorandum on 'The Jewish
Question', 25 January 1939

How the Nazis themselves weighed up their Jewish policy and its central significance in the drama of 1938 can be assessed in this revealing extract from a German Foreign Ministry memorandum on 'The Jewish Question', dated 25 January 1939:

Subject: The Jewish Question as a Factor in Foreign Policy in 1938

1. Germany's Jewish policy as condition and consequence of foreign policy decisions in 1938.
2. The aim of German Jewish policy: emigration.
3. Means, ways and destinations of Jewish emigration.
4. The Jewish émigré as the best propaganda for Germany's Jewish policy.

It is probably no coincidence that the fateful year of 1938 brought not only the realization of the concept of a Greater Germany, but at the same time has brought the Jewish Question close to solution. For the Jewish policy was both pre-condition and consequence of the events of 1938. More than the power politics and hostility of the former enemy in the World War it was the penetration of Jewish influence and the corrupting Jewish mentality in politics, economy and culture which paralysed the strength and the will of the German people to rise once more . . .

But the need for a radical solution of the Jewish question also resulted from the developments in foreign affairs which added 200,000 persons of the Jewish faith in Austria to the 500,000 living in the old Reich. The influence of the Jews in the Austrian economy made it necessary to take immediate steps to eliminate the Jews from the German economy . . .

The campaign launched in reprisal for the assassination of Secretary of Legation vom Rath has speeded up this process so greatly that Jewish retail trade – so far with the exception of foreign-owned stores – has vanished completely from our streets. The liquidation of Jewish wholesale and manufacturing enterprises, and of houses and real estate owned by Jews, is gradually progressing so far that within a limited period of time the existence of Jewish property will in Germany be a thing of the past . . .

The ultimate aim of Germany's policy is the emigration of all Jews living in German territory . . . The Jew has been eliminated from politics and culture, but until 1938 his powerful economic position in Germany and his tenacious determination to hold out until the return of 'better times' remained unbroken . . .

But the Jew had underestimated the consistency and strength of the National-Socialist idea.

The . . . question, to which countries the organized emigration of the Jews should be directed, could [not] be solved . . . by the Evian Conference; each of the countries taking part expressed its agreement in principle to help solve the refugee problem, but declared that it was unable to accept large masses of Jewish emigres into its territory. While in the years 1933–4 more than 100,000 Jews from Germany made their way abroad, legally or illegally, and were able to gain a foothold in a new host nation, either with the aid of relatives living abroad, or the pity of humanitarian circles, by now almost all countries in the world have sealed their borders hermetically against the burdensome Jewish intruders . . .

Even the migration of only about 100,000 Jews has been sufficient to waken the interest in, if not the understanding of, the Jewish danger in many countries, and it can be foreseen that the Jewish question will develop into an international political problem when large numbers of Jews from Germany, Poland, Hungary and Rumania are set in motion by the increasing pressure of their host nations. Even for Germany the Jewish question will not be solved when the last Jew has left German soil . . .

Palestine, which has already been designated by a popular catchword as the target of emigration, cannot be considered as such because its absorptive capacity for a mass influx of Jews is insufficient. Under pressure of Arab resistance the British Mandatory government has limited Jewish immigration into Palestine to a minimum.

At first the emigration of German Jews to Palestine received extensive support from Germany through the conclusion of an agreement with Jewish representatives in Palestine . . . But Germany is obliged to discern the danger in the creation of a Jewish State, which even in a miniature form could provide world Jewry with a basis for action similar to that of the Vatican State for political Catholicism, and could absorb only a fraction of the Jews. The realization that Jewry will always be the implacable enemy of the Third Reich forces us to the decision to prevent any strengthening of the Jewish position. A Jewish State would give world Jewry increased power in international law and relations . . .

Germany has an important interest in seeing the splintering of Jewry maintained. Those who argue that this will cause the creation of sources of boycott and anti-German centres all over the world disregard a development already evident, that the influx of Jews arouses the resistance of the native population in all parts of the world and thus provides the best propaganda for Germany's policy towards the Jews.

In North America, in South America, in France, in Holland, Scandinavia and Greece – wherever the stream of Jewish migrants has poured in, a clear increase in anti-Semitism has already been recorded. It must be the aim of German foreign policy to strengthen this wave of anti-Semitism . . .

The poorer the Jewish immigrant is and the greater the burden he constitutes for the country into which he has immigrated, the stronger the reaction will be in the host country, and the more desirable the effect in support of German propaganda. The aim of this German policy is a future international solution of the Jewish question, dictated not by false pity for a 'Jewish religious minority that has been driven out' but by the mature realisation by all nations of the nature of the danger that Jewry spells for the national character of the nations.

Source: Excerpted from Document 58 in Yitzhak Arad, Yisrael Gutman and Abraham Margaliot (eds), Documents on the Holocaust: Selected Sources on the Destruction of the Jews of Germany and Austria, Poland, and the Soviet Union *(Yad Vashem Publications, 1981)*

Hitler threatens Jews with annihilation 9

Hitler's dream of a Europe 'purified' of Jews was expressed in a surprisingly open and threatening way in a speech he delivered to the German Parliament on 30 January 1939:

In connection with the Jewish question I have this to say: it is a shameful spectacle to see how the whole democratic world is oozing sympathy for the poor tormented Jewish people, but remains hard-hearted and obdurate when it comes to helping them . . .

The world has sufficient space for settlements but we must once and for all get rid of the opinion that the Jewish race was only created by God for the purpose of being . . . a parasite living on the body and the productive work of other nations. The Jewish race will have to adapt itself to sound constructive activity as other nations do, or sooner or later it will succumb to a crisis of an inconceivable magnitude.

One thing I should like to say on this day which may be memorable for others as well as for us Germans: in the course of my life I have very often been a prophet, and have usually been ridiculed for it. During the time of my struggle for power it was in the first instance the Jewish race which received my prophecies with laughter when I said that I would one day take over the leadership of the State, and with it that of the whole nation, and that I would then settle the whole Jewish problem. The laughter was uproarious, but I think that for some time now they have been laughing on the other side of their face.

TODAY I WILL ONCE MORE BE A PROPHET: IF THE INTERNATIONAL JEWISH FINANCIERS IN AND OUTSIDE EUROPE SHOULD SUCCEED IN PLUNGING THE NATIONS ONCE MORE INTO A WORLD WAR, THEN THE RESULT WILL NOT BE

THE BOLSHEVIZATION OF THE EARTH, AND THUS THE VICTORY OF JEWRY, BUT THE ANNIHILATION OF THE JEWISH RACE IN EUROPE!

Source: Yitzhak Arad, Yisrael Gutman and Abraham Margaliot (eds), Documents on the Holocaust: Selected Sources on the Destruction of the Jews of Germany and Austria, Poland, and the Soviet Union, *(Yad Vashem Publications, 1981), Document 59*

10 Reinhard Heydrich's Order, 21 September 1939

During the early days of the Second World War, Reinhard Heydrich, Head of the Reich Security Main Office and of the Security Police, was given the responsibility of devising a systematic interim method of dealing with the Jews in occupied Poland until a more permanent solution could be found. On 21 September 1939 Heydrich issued the following instructions to the leaders of the *Einsatzgruppen* (the *Einsatzgruppen* were special 'task forces' [i.e. death squads] of the Security Police which operated behind the German front-line troops). They would later play a murderous role in shooting to death over two million civilians – including an estimated 1.5 million Jews in territory taken from the Russians.

The subject of his directive was 'the Jewish question in the occupied territory' of Poland and established the basis for the organization, concentration and ghettoization of Jews that would define Jewish life in Poland until the death camps were ready to receive them:

I refer to the conference held in Berlin today, and again point out that the *planned total measures* (i.e. the final aim) are to be kept *strictly secret*.

A distinction must be made between:

1. the final aim (which will require extended periods of time) and
2. the stages leading to the fulfilment of this final aim . . .

The planned measures require the *most thorough preparation* with regard to technical as well as economic aspects.

It is obvious that the tasks ahead . . . cannot be laid down in full detail . . .

For the time being, the first prerequisite for the final aim is the concentration of the Jews from the countryside into the larger cities. This is to be carried out speedily . . .

In this connection it should be borne in mind that only cities which are rail junctions, or are at least located on railroad lines, should be selected as concentration points.

On principle, Jewish communities of less than 500 persons are to be dissolved and transferred to the nearest concentration centre ...

II
Councils of Jewish Elders

1. In each Jewish community a Council of Jewish Elders is to be set up which, as far as possible, is to be composed of the remaining authoritative personalities and rabbis ... The Council is to be made *fully responsible*, in the literal sense of the word, for the exact and prompt implementation of directives already issued or to be issued in the future.
2. In case of sabotage of such instructions, the Councils are to be warned that the most severe measures will be taken.
3. The Jewish Councils are to carry out an approximate census of the Jews in their areas ...
4. ... The reason to be given for the concentration in the cities is that the Jews have taken a decisive part in sniper attacks and plundering.
5. ... the concentration of the Jews in the cities will probably call for regulations in these cities which will forbid their entry to certain quarters completely and that ... they may, for instance, not leave the ghetto, nor leave their homes after a certain hour in the evening, etc.

Source: Yitzhak Arad, Yisrael Gutman and Abraham Margaliot (eds), Documents on the Holocaust: Selected Sources on the Destruction of the Jews of Germany and Austria, Poland, and the Soviet Union *(Yad Vashem Publications, 1981), Document 73*

The Warsaw Ghetto: The Jewish response

11

The horrific implications of Nazi rule for the Jews of Poland were understood in the following way by a contemporary Warsaw Jewish chronicler, Chaim Kaplan. Yet he also believed, quite prophetically, in the indomitability of the Jewish spirit.

March 10, 1940
The gigantic catastrophe which has descended on Polish Jewry has no parallel, even in the darkest periods of Jewish history. Firstly – the depth of the hatred. This is not hatred whose source is simply in a party platform, invented for political purposes.

It is a hatred of emotion, whose source is some psychopathic disease. In its outward manifestation it appears as physiological hatred, which sees the object of its hatred as tainted in body, as lepers who have no place in society ... It is our good fortune that the conquerors failed to understand the nature and strength of Polish Jewry. Logically, we are obliged to die. According to the laws of nature, our end is destruction and total annihilation. How can an entire community feed itself when it has no grip on life? For there is no occupation, no trade which is not limited and circumscribed for us.

But even this time we did not comply with the laws of nature. There is within us some hidden power, mysterious and secret, which keeps us going, keeps us alive, despite the natural law. If we cannot live on what is permitted, we live on what is forbidden ...

The Jews of Poland – oppressed and broken, shamed and debased, still love life, and do not wish to leave this world before their time. Say what you like, the will to live amidst terrible suffering is the manifestation of some hidden power whose nature we do not yet know. It is a marvellous, life-preserving power ... The fact that we have hardly any suicides is worthy of special emphasis.

We have remained naked. But as long as that secret power is concealed within us, we shall not yield to despair. The strength of this power lies in the very nature of the Polish Jew, which is rooted in our eternal tradition that commands us to live.

Source: Yitzhak Arad, Yisrael Gutman and Abraham Marguliot (eds), Documents on the Holocaust: Selected Sources on the Destruction of the Jews of Germany and Austria, Poland, and the Soviet Union *(Yad Vashem Publications, 1981), Document 88*

12 The Wannsee Conference

On 20 January 1942, a conference was convened beside Lake Wannsee in Berlin. Its purpose was to coordinate the activities of all bodies and organizations whose participation would be needed for the 'Final Solution'. Although the key decisions had clearly already been reached at the highest levels of government, this conference is highly significant because Heydrich (who chaired the meeting) was able to gain unchallenged administrative supremacy for the SS in all matters relating to the implementation of Holocaust policy. Seated at this meeting were highly educated and cultivated Germans from many different branches of government – the cream of the German leadership. They calmly and deliberately listened to plans for the annihilation of an entire people.

3 Jews marked out for death, 20 January 1942

This document makes it abundantly clear that the Nazis were, by the beginning of 1942, unswervingly committed to killing every single Jew (according to their estimate 11 million) on the continent of Europe, including those living in countries that were neutral, for example Eire, Sweden, Switzerland and Spain, or not yet conquered and occupied, for example Great Britain and the central and eastern regions of the Soviet Union.

A copy of the minutes of the conference, prepared by Adolf Eichmann, has survived intact. It constitutes one of the most important documents on the history of the Holocaust. The following is an excerpt:

In view of the dangers of emigration in war-time, and the possibilities in the East, the Reichsführer SS and Chief of the German Police (Himmler) has forbidden the emigration of Jews.

Emigration has now been replaced by evacuation of the Jews to the East, as a further possible solution, with the appropriate prior authorization of the Führer.

However, this operation should be regarded only as a provisional option; but it is already supplying practical experience of great significance in view of the coming final solution of the Jewish question.

In the course of this final solution of the European Jewish question approximately 11 million Jews may be taken into consideration, distributed over the individual countries as follows:

	Country	Number
A.	Germany	131,800
	Austria	43,700
	Eastern Territories	420,000
	General Government (i.e. central Poland)	2,284,000
	Bialystok	400,000
	Protectorate of Bohemia and Moravia	74,200
	Estonia – free of Jews	
	Latvia	3,500
	Lithuania	34,000
	Belgium	43,000
	Denmark	5,600
	France: Occupied territory	165,000
	France: Unoccupied territory	700,000
	Greece	69,600
	Holland	160,800
	Norway	1,300
B.	Bulgaria	48,000
	England	330,000
	Finland	2,300
	Ireland	4,000
	Italy, including Sardinia	58,000
	Albania	200
	Croatia	40,000
	Portugal	3,000
	Rumania, including Bessarabia	342,000
	Sweden	8,000
	Switzerland	18,000
	Serbia	10,000
	Slovakia	88,000
	Spain	6,000
	Turkey (European portion)	55,500
	Hungary	742,800
	USSR	5,000,000
	Ukraine	2,994,684
	White Russia, without Bialystok	446,484
	Total:	over 11,000,000

The Jews are to be utilized for work in the East in an expedient manner in the course of the final solution. In large (labour) columns, with the sexes separated, Jews capable of work will be moved into those areas as they build roads, during which a large proportion will no doubt drop out through natural reduction. The remnant that eventually remains will require suitable treatment; because it will without doubt represent the most (physically) resistant part, it consists of a natural selection that could, on its release, become the germ-cell of a new Jewish revival (witness the experience of history).

Europe is to be combed through from West to East in the course of the practical implementation of the final solution . . .

The evacuated Jews will first be taken, group by group, to so-called transit ghettos, in order to be transported further east from there.

Source: Excerpted from Yitzhak Arad, Yisrael Gutman and Abraham Margaliot (eds), Documents on the Holocaust: Selected Sources on the Destruction of the Jews of Germany and Austria, Poland, and the Soviet Union *(Yad Vashem Publications, 1981), Document 117*

The *Einsatzgruppen* death squads: An 13
eyewitness account

Over one million Jews were shot to death during the first 15 months of Nazi Germany's campaign in the Soviet Union, following the launch of Operation Barbarossa on 22 June 1941. At the Nuremberg Trials of 1945 the following graphic account of one such massacre was given by a German builder, Hermann Gräbe:

A few lorries were parked in front of the mounds from which people were being driven by armed Ukrainian militia under the supervision of an armed SS man. The militia provided the guards on the lorries and drove them to and from the ditch. All these people wore the prescribed yellow patches on the front and back of their clothing so that they were identifiable as Jews . . .

I could now hear a series of rifle shots from behind the mounds. The people who had got off the lorries – men, women and children of all ages – had to undress on the orders of an SS man who was carrying a riding or dog whip in his hand. They had to place their clothing on separate piles for shoes, clothing and under-wear. I saw a pile of shoes containing approximately 800–1,000 pairs, and great heaps of underwear and clothing. Without weeping or crying out these people undressed and stood together in family groups, embracing each other and saying goodbye while waiting for a sign from another SS man who stood on the edge of the ditch and also had a whip. During the quarter of an hour in which I stood near the ditch I did not hear a single complaint or plea for mercy. I watched a family of about eight, a man and a woman, both about fifty-years-old with their children of about one, eight and ten, as well as two grown-up daughters of about twenty and twenty-four. An old woman with snow-white hair held a one-year-old child in her arms singing to it and tickling it. The child squeaked with delight. The married couple looked on with tears in their eyes. The father held the ten-year-old boy by the hand speaking softly to him. The boy was struggling to hold back his tears. The father pointed a finger to the sky and stroked his head and seemed to be explaining something to him. At this moment, the SS man near the ditch called out something to his comrade. The latter counted off some twenty people and ordered them behind the mound. The family of which I have just spoken was among them. I can still remember how a girl, slender and dark, pointed to herself as she went past me, saying, 'twenty-three'.

I walked round the mound and stood in front of the huge grave. The bodies were lying so tightly packed together that only their heads showed, from almost all of which blood ran down over their shoulders. Some were still moving. Others raised their hands and turned their heads to show they were still alive. The ditch was already three-quarters full. I estimate that it already held about a thousand bodies. I turned my eyes towards the man doing the shooting. He was an SS man; he sat, legs swinging, on the edge of the ditch. He had an automatic rifle resting on his knees and he was smoking a cigarette. The people, completely naked, climbed down steps which had been cut into the clay wall of the ditch, stumbled over the heads of those lying there and stopped at the spot indicated by the SS man. They lay down on top of the dead and wounded; some stroked those still living and spoke quietly to them. Then I heard a series of rifle shots. I looked into the ditch and saw the bodies contorting or, the heads already inert, sinking on the corpses beneath. Blood flowed from the nape of their necks. I was surprised not to be ordered away, but I noticed three postmen in uniform standing nearby. Then the next batch came up, climbed down into the ditch, laid themselves next to the previous victims and were shot . . .

I am making the above statement in Wiesbaden, Germany on 10 November 1945. I swear to God it is the whole truth.

Source: Jeremy Noakes and Geoffrey Pridham, Nazism 1919–1945. A Documentary Reader, *Vol. III (Exeter University Press, 1988), Document 823*

Appeal to the outside world 14

The Jewish Labour Bund, which had enjoyed massive pre-war support among the Jews of Poland, strove to maintain its political activities underground. It was represented in the Polish Government-in-exile in London and liaised, wherever possible, with the Polish underground in Warsaw and elsewhere in Poland. The following appeal, made in May 1942, is a poignant example of one of its attempts to communicate the agony of Poland's Jews to its overseas contacts, in this case urging the Polish Government-in-exile to take immediate action.

From the day the Russo-German war broke out, the Germans undertook the physical extermination of the Jewish population on Polish territory, using for that purpose Ukrainians and Lithuanian Siauliai [fascist paramilitary police units]. It began first of all in Eastern Galicia in the summer months of 1941. Their method everywhere was as follows: men from 14 to 60 were slaughtered, machine-gunned, or killed by hand grenades. They had to dig their own graves first. Children in orphanages, inmates of old-age homes, and the hospitalised sick were shot, women were killed on the streets. In many towns Jews were taken away to an 'unknown destination' and executed in the nearby woods. 30,000 Jews were murdered in Lwow, 15,000 in Stanlawow, 5,000 in Tarnopol, 2,000 in Zloczow, 4,000 in Brzezany (the town had 18,000 Jews, now has 1,700). The same happened in Zborow, Kolomyja . . . and [many] other places.

The extermination actions in those towns recurred repeatedly in many towns: they are still going on . . .

In October and November the same thing began to happen in Vilna, the Vilna area and Lithuanian Kovno. In Vilna 50,000 Jews were murdered during November. There are now 12,000 Jews, in Vilna. According to various estimates, the number of Jews bestially murdered in the Vilna regions and Lithuanian Kovno is put at 300,000 . . .

In November and December, the annihilation action was begun in the Polish territory incorporated into the Reich, i.e. *Warthegau*. The annihilation was carried out by means of gassing, which took place in the village of Chelmno, 12 km. from Kolo. A special van [gas chamber] was used, in which 90 people were loaded. The victims were buried in special graves in a clearing in the Lubard Forest. The graves were dug by the victims themselves. On average, 1,000 people were gassed daily. Between November 1941 and March 1942 . . . 35,000 Jews from the Lodz ghetto, as well as a certain number of Gypsies, were gassed in Chelmno.

In February 1942, the annihilation of Jews in the territory which is called the General Government was started. The beginning: Tarnow and Radom, where Gestapo and SS men began visiting the Jewish districts daily, systematically killing Jews in the streets, courtyards and houses. In March, a mass action began in Lublin of deporting all Jews from the city. Children and old people, in the orphanage and old-age homes and also the patients in the general hospital and the hospital for contagious diseases, were bestially put to death, and also many people were killed in the streets and in their homes. The total number of victims was over 2,000. Some 25,000 Jews were taken from Lublin in sealed railroad cars to an 'unknown destination', after which every trace of them has disappeared. Some 3,000 Jews were confined in barracks in Majdanek Tatarowy, a suburb of Lublin. Not a single Jew is left in Lublin today. In the last days of March in Cracow, fifty Jews were rounded up, from a list prepared beforehand, and were shot in the yards in front of their homes. In Warsaw, in the night of April 17/18, the Gestapo organised a blood bath in the ghetto. According to a prepared list, they dragged out more than fifty Jews, men and women, from their homes and murdered them in front of their buildings. Many were not found at home. Starting with April 18, even in broad daylight, they kill a few Jews a day in their homes and on the streets. This action is conducted with prepared lists, comprising all strata of Jews in the Warsaw ghetto. There is talk of bloody nights to come. To date the Germans have murdered an estimated 700,000 Polish Jews.

The above facts confirm irrefutably that the criminal German government has undertaken to carry out Hitler's prophecy that five minutes before the war ends, however it ends, he would annihilate all the Jews in Europe. We firmly believe that Hitler's Germans will at the proper time be presented with an appropriate reckoning for their atrocities and bestialities. For the Jewish population, which now endures an inconceivable hell, this is not consolation enough. Millions of Polish citizens of Jewish nationality are threatened with imminent extermination.

We therefore turn to the Government of Poland, as custodian and representative of the whole population living on Polish soil, immediately to take the necessary steps to prevent the annihilation of Polish Jewry. To that end, the Government of Poland should bring all its influence to bear on the governments of the Allied Powers and on all authoritative circles in those countries so that they will, without delay, apply a policy of retribution against German citizens and the fifth columnists living in the countries of the Allied Powers. The Government of Poland and the governments of the Allied Powers should notify the German government as to the application of retribution. It should be made aware that Germans in the United States and in other countries will even now be answering for the bestial annihilation of the Jewish population.

We realise that we are asking the Government of Poland to take extraordinary measures. This is the only possibility of rescuing millions of Jews from certain annihilation.

Source: Excerpt from copy of original housed in YIVO Archives, cited in Lucy Dawidowicz, A Holocaust Reader *(Behrman House, 1976), pp. 316–18*

Inside the mind of a perpetrator 15

Case No. 1: A letter home from the Russian 'Front'

Crude prejudice, naked fanaticism and bloodlust were often satisfied in those who formed part of the killing squads. What follows is an extract from a letter written by a German police-sergeant serving in an EinsatzKommando unit in the southern Ukraine:

We men of the new Germany must be strict with ourselves even if it means a long period of separation from our family. For we must finish matters once and for all and finally settle accounts with the war criminals, in order to create a better and eternal Germany for our heirs. We are not sleeping here. There are three or four operations a week. Sometimes Gypsies, another time Jews, partisans and all sorts of trash ... We are not carrying on a lawless regime here, but when an action requires immediate atonement we contact the SD and justice takes its course. If the official judicial system were operating, it would be impossible to exterminate a whole family when only the father is guilty.

I do not know if you ... ever saw such frightful kinds of Jews in Poland. I am grateful for having been allowed to see this bastard race close up. If fate permits, I shall have something to tell my children. Syphilitics, cripples, idiots were typical of them. One thing was clear: they were materialists to the end. They were saying things like: 'We are skilled workers, you are not going to shoot us.' They were not men but monkeys in human form.

Ah well, there is only a small percentage of the 24,000 Jews of Kamenetz-Podolsk left. The Yids in the surrounding area are also clients of ours. We are ruthlessly making a clean sweep with a clear conscience and then ... the waves close over, the world has peace.

Source: Jeremy Noakes And Geoffrey Pridham, Nazism 1919–1945. A Documentary Reader, *Vol. III (Exeter University Press, 1988), Document 912*

Case No. 2: The diary of SS Dr Johann Paul Kremer

Especially perplexing and disturbing is the behaviour of the SS doctors, some of whom performed grisly experiments on human guinea-pigs in the camps. They tended to justify their endeavours as contributions to the advance of medical knowledge. Such 'medical' activity involved sterilization, castration, the removal of living foetuses at different stages of development, transplanting human organs, seeing how long a man could survive in freezing water and many other experiments besides. The following excerpt is taken from the diaries of SS Doctor Johann Kremer, Professor of Medicine at the University of Münster and assigned to the death camp at Auschwitz for only ten weeks.

2 September, 1942 – First time present at a special action at 3 a.m. Compared with this, Dante's Inferno seems to me a comedy. Not for nothing is Auschwitz called the 'extermination camp'!

5 September, 1942 – This afternoon present at a special action for prisoners in the female camp: horror of horrors. Dr Thilo is right when he told me this morning that we are in the 'anus mundi'. In the evening, at approximately eight, I was again present at a special action for the Dutch. The men all want to take part in these actions because of the special rations they get, consisting of a fifth of a litre of schnapps, 5 cigarettes, 100 g. of sausage and bread.

6 September, 1942 – Today, Sunday, excellent lunch: tomato soup, half a hen with potatoes and red cabbage (20 g. fat) sweets and marvellous vanilla ice . . . in the evening at eight outside for a special action.

9 September, 1942 – This morning I got the pleasant news from my lawyer . . . that I got divorced from my wife on the first of the month (Note: I see colours again, a black curtain is drawn from my life). Later on present at a corporal punishment of eight prisoners and an execution by shooting with small calibre rifles. Got soap flakes and two pieces of soap . . . In the evening present at a special action for the fourth time.

23 September, 1942 – Present last night at the sixth and seventh special actions . . . In the evening dinner in the commandant's house . . . a real banquet. We had apple pie, as much as we wanted, good coffee, excellent beer and cakes.

3 October, 1942 – Today we fixed living material of human liver, spleen and pancreas . . .

12 October, 1942 – Inoculation against typhoid, after that feverish in the evening. In spite of that, present at a special action during the night (1,600 people from Holland). Terrible scenes near the last bunker. The tenth special action.

13 November, 1942 – Living, fresh material of liver, spleen and pancreas taken from a Jewish prisoner of 18 years of age, who was very atrophic. First we took a photo of him. Liver and spleen fixed as usual in Carnoy and pancreas in Zenker (prisoner no. 68030).

Source: Elie Cohen, Human Behaviour in the Concentration Camp *(W. Norton, 1953)*

Case No. 3: Heinrich Himmler, Head of the SS

SS Leader Heinrich Himmler, who had almost fainted when he attended a mass execution at Minsk, was nevertheless able to deliver the following address to senior SS officers in Poznan on 4 October 1943. There are two emphases in his speech, first the need for absolute secrecy in this 'glorious' task and secondly his insistence that the 'honour' of the SS remain unsullied:

I also want to speak to you here, in complete frankness, of a really grave chapter. Amongst ourselves, for once, it shall be said quite openly, but all the same we will never speak about it in public . . . I am referring here to the evacuation of the Jews, the extermination of the Jewish people. This is one of the things that is easily said: 'The Jewish people are going to be exterminated,' that's what every Party member says, 'sure, it's in our programme, elimination of the Jews, extermination – it'll be done.' And then they all come along, the 80 million worthy Germans, and each one has his one decent Jew. Of course, the others are swine, but this one, he is a first-rate Jew. Of all those who talk like that, not one has seen it happen, not one has had to go through with it. Most of you men know what it is like to see 100 corpses side by side, or 500 or 1,000. To have stood fast through this and – except for cases of human weakness – to have stayed decent, that has made us hard. This is an unwritten and never-to-be-written page of glory in our history . . .

The wealth they possessed we took from them. I gave a strict order . . . that this wealth will of course be handed over to the Reich in its entirety. We have taken none of it for ourselves. Individuals, who have erred will be punished in accordance with the order given by me at the start that anyone who takes so much as a single Mark of this money is a dead man. A number of SS men – they are not very many – committed this offence, and they shall die. There will be no mercy. We had the moral right, we had the duty towards our people, to destroy this people that wanted to destroy us. But we do not have the right to enrich ourselves by so much as a fur, as a watch, by one Mark or a cigarette or anything else. We do not want, in the end, because we destroyed a bacillus, to be infected by this bacillus and to die. I will never stand by and watch while even a small rotten spot develops or takes hold. Wherever it may form we will together burn it away. All in all, however, we can say that we have carried out this most difficult of tasks in a spirit of love for our people. And we have suffered no harm to our inner being, our soul, our character.

Source: Yitzhak Arad, Yisrael Gutman and Abraham Margaliot (eds), Documents on the Holocaust: Selected Sources on the Destruction of the Jews of Germany and Austria, Poland, and the Soviet Union *(Yad Vashem Publications, 1981), Document 161*

Case no. 4: Rudolf Hoess, Commandant of Auschwitz

The following three documents are drawn from the startling reminiscences, rationalizations and self-evaluation of Rudolf Hoess. For three blood-drenched years Hoess was the Commandant at Auschwitz, where he oversaw the slaughter of more than two million people. He was himself executed at Auschwitz in 1947.

a) In the summer of 1941 – I cannot remember the exact date – I was suddenly summoned to the Reichsführer SS . . . Contrary to his usual custom, Himmler received me without his adjutant being present and said in effect:

'The Führer has ordered that the Jewish question be solved once and for all and that we, the SS, are to implement that order.

'The existing extermination centres in the East are not in a position to carry out the large actions which are anticipated. I have therefore earmarked Auschwitz for this purpose, both because of its good position as regards communications and because the area can easily be isolated and camouflaged . . . It is difficult and onerous and calls for complete devotion notwithstanding the difficulties which may arise . . .

'You will treat this order as absolutely secret, even from your superiors. After your talk with Eichmann you will immediately forward to me the plans of the projected installations.

'The Jews are the sworn enemies of the German people and must be eradicated. Every Jew that we can lay our hands on is to be destroyed now during the war, without exception. If we cannot now obliterate the biological basis of Jewry, the Jews will one day destroy the German people.'

b) I must emphasize here that I have never personally hated the Jews. It is true that I looked upon them as the enemies of our people. But just because of this I saw no difference between them and the other prisoners, and I treated them all in the same way. I never drew any distinctions. In any event the emotion of hatred is foreign to my nature. But I know what hate is, and what it looks like. I have seen it and I have suffered it myself . . .

When in the summer of 1941 Himmler gave me the order to prepare installations at Auschwitz where mass exterminations could take place, and personally to carry out these exterminations, I did not have the slightest idea of their scale or consequences. It was certainly an extraordinary and monstrous order. Nevertheless the reasons behind the extermination programme seemed to me right. I did not reflect on it at the time.

I had been given an order, and I had to carry it out. Whether this mass extermination of the Jews was necessary or not was something on which I could not allow myself to form an opinion, for I lacked the necessary breadth of view.

When asked if he had ever regarded the Jews he butchered as guilty of any crime or in any way deserving of their fate, Hoess attempted to explain that the question was in some way inappropriate as he had been living in a totally different reality.

c) Don't you see, we SS men were not supposed to think about these things; it never even occurred to us. And besides, it was something already taken for granted that the Jews were to blame for everything . . . We just never heard anything else. It was not just newspapers like the Stürmer but it was everything we ever heard.

Even our military and ideological training took for granted that we had to protect Germany from the Jews ... It only started to occur to me after the collapse that maybe it was not all quite right, after I heard what everybody was saying. But nobody had ever said these things before: at least we never heard of it.

Now I wonder if Himmler really believed all that himself or just gave me an excuse to justify what he wanted me to do. But, anyway, that really didn't matter. We were all so trained to obey orders without even thinking that the thought of disobeying an order would simply never have occurred to anybody and somebody else would have done just as well if I hadn't ... Himmler was so strict about little things, and executed SS men for such small offences, that naturally we took it for granted that he was acting according to a strict code of honour ...

You can be sure that it was not always a pleasure to see those mountains of corpses or smell the continual burning. But Himmler had ordered it and had explained the necessity and I really never gave much thought to whether it was wrong. It just seemed a necessity.

Sources: a) & b) Commandant of Auschwitz: The Autobiography of Rudolf Hoess *(Weidenfeld and Nicolson, 1959); c) Gustav Gilbert,* Nuremberg Diary *(Farrar, Straus & Giroux, 1974)*

The victims: Defiant responses 16

a) The following proclamation, calling for resistance, was issued in January, 1942 in the ghetto of Vilna, Lithuania, by the Jewish Pioneer Youth Group:

Jewish youth, do not be led astray. Of the 80,000 Jews in the 'Jerusalem of Lithuania' (Vilna) only 20,000 have remained. Before our eyes they tore from us our parents, our brothers and sisters. Where are the hundreds of men who were taken away for work by the Lithuanian 'snatchers'? Where are the naked women and children who were taken from us in the night of terror of the 'provokatzia'?

Where are the Jews (who were taken away) on the Day of Atonement?

Where are our brothers from the second ghetto?

All those who were taken away from the ghetto never came back.

All the roads of the Gestapo lead to Ponary.

And Ponary is death!

Doubters! Cast off all illusions. Your children, your husbands and your wives are no longer alive.

Ponary is not a camp — all are shot there.

Hitler aims to destroy all the Jews of Europe. The Jews of Lithuania are fated to be the first in line.

Let us not go as sheep to slaughter!

It is true that we are weak and defenceless, but resistance is the only reply to the enemy!

Brothers! It is better to fall as free fighters than to live by the grace of the murderers.

Resist! To the last breath.

Source: Yitzhak Arad, Yisrael Gutman and Abraham Margaliot (eds), Documents on the Holocaust: Selected Sources on the Destruction of the Jews of Germany and Austria, Poland, and the Soviet Union *(Yad Vashem Publications, 1981), Document 196*

b) The following call to armed self-defence was made to the Jewish population of Warsaw in a *Ha-Shomer Ha-Zair* (Zionist movement) article which appeared in a Warsaw undergound publication, *Jutrznia* ('Dawn'), on 28 March 1942.

We know that Hitler's system of murder, slaughter and robbery leads steadily to a dead end and the destruction of the Jews. The fate of the Jews in the Soviet Russian areas occupied by the Germans, and in the Warthegau [areas of western Poland annexed to German Reich] marks a new period in the total annihilation of the Jewish population. The huge murder machine has been turned against Jewish masses that are weak, unarmed, brought low by hunger, camps and deportations. With satanic methods it liquidates the Jewish population centres one by one. The victory over the Jews will have to serve the Germans as recompense for the losses they have suffered at the front. Spilling the blood of defenceless Jews will have to take the place of Hitler's great dreams that failed to come true.

We also know that the march of Hitler's troops has been halted by the heroic Red Army and that the Spring Offensive will see the beginning of the far-reaching destruction of the Nazis in Europe. For the Jewish masses this will be a period of greater bloodshed than any in their history. There is no doubt that when Hitler feels that the end of his rule is approaching he will seek to drown the Jews in a sea of blood. Jewish youth must prepare in the face of those difficult days. There must therefore be a start to the recruiting of all creative forces among the Jews. For generation upon generation passivity and lack of faith in our own strength had pressed upon us; but our history also shows beautiful pages glowing with heroism and struggle. *It is our duty to join this period of heroism.*

Source: Yitzhak Arad, Yisrael Gutman and Abraham Margaliot (eds), Documents on the Holocaust: Selected Sources on the Destruction of the Jews of Germany and Austria, Poland, and the Soviet Union *(Yad Vashem Publications, 1981), Document 125*

c) Despite the hopelessness of most forms of Jewish armed resistance, what it meant to those who took part can be gauged from the following document. It is taken from the last letter written by Mordechai Anielewicz, the leader of the Warsaw Ghetto uprising.

It is impossible to put into words what we have been through. One thing is clear, what happened exceeded our boldest dreams. The Germans ran twice from the ghetto. One of our companies held out for 40 minutes and another for more than 6 hours . . . Several of our companies attacked the dispersing Germans . . . Y(echiel) fell. He fell a hero, at the machine gun. I feel that great things are happening and what we dared do is of great, enormous importance . . .

It is impossible to describe the conditions under which the Jews of the ghetto are now living. Only a few will be able to hold out. The remainder will die sooner or later. Their fate is decided. In almost all the hiding places in which thousands are concealing themselves it is not possible to light a candle for lack of air.

With the aid of our transmitter we heard a marvellous report on our fighting . . . The fact that we are remembered beyond the ghetto walls encourages us in our struggle. Peace go with you, my friend! . . . The dream of my life has risen to become fact. Self-defence in the ghetto will have become a reality. Jewish armed resistance and revenge are facts. I have been a witness to the magnificent, heroic fighting of Jewish men in battle.

Ghetto, April 23 1943

Source: Yitzhak Arad, Yisrael Gutman and Abraham Margaliot (eds), Documents on the Holocaust: Selected Sources on the Destruction of the Jews of Germany and Austria, Poland, and the Soviet Union *(Yad Vashem Publications, 1981), Document 145 (written to Yitzhak Cukierman, a leader of the Pioneer Underground in occupied Poland and representative of the Jewish Fighting Organisation on the Aryan side in Warsaw)*

Spiritual resistance 17

a) The following extract, taken from the Warsaw Ghetto diary of Avraham Levin, demonstrates not only the intrinsic importance of recording and remembering but – in such tragic circumstances and against all the odds – the intensity of the Jewish commitment to life and survival:

One of the most surprising side-effects of this war is the clinging to life, the almost total absence of suicides. People die in great numbers of starvation, the typhus epidemic or dysentery, they are tortured and murdered by the Germans in great numbers, but they do not escape from life by their own desire. On the contrary, they are tied to life by all their senses, they want to live at any price and to survive the war. The tensions of this historic world conflict are so great that all wish to see the outcome of the gigantic struggle and the new regime in the world, the small and the great, old men and boys. The old have just one wish: the privilege of seeing the end and surviving Hitler.

I know a Jew who is all old age. He is certainly about 80. Last winter a great tragedy befell the old man. He had an only son who was about 52. The son died of typhus. He has no other children. And the son died of typhus. He has no other children. And the son died. He did not marry a second time and lived with his son. A few days ago I visited the old man. When I left – his mind is still entirely clear – he burst out crying and said: 'I want to see the end of the war, even if I live only another half an hour!'

Why should the old man wish so much to stay alive? There it is: even he wants to live, 'if only for half an hour' after the last shot is fired. That is the burning desire of all the Jews.

Source: Yitzhak Arad, Yisrael Gutman and Abraham Margaliot (eds), Documents on the Holocaust: Selected Sources on the Destruction of the Jews of Germany and Austria, Poland, and the Soviet Union *(Yad Vashem Publications, 1981), Document 89*

b) Some Jews, faced with imminent death, wished to preserve the memory of their terrible fate for future generations. Israel Lichtenstein, a teacher of Yiddish, set out his last will and testament during the eleventh day of a 'resettlement' action in Warsaw. In it he displays not only resignation but a desperate wish that he and his family be remembered.

With zeal and zest I threw myself into the work to help assemble archive materials. I was entrusted to be the custodian; I hid the material. Besides me, no one knew. I confided only in my friend Hersh Wasser, my superior.

It is well hidden. Please God that it be preserved. That will be the finest and best that we achieved in the present gruesome time.

I know that we will not endure. To survive and remain alive [after] such horrible murders and massacres is impossible. Therefore I write this testament of mine. Perhaps I am not worthy of being remembered, but just for my grit in working with the society 'Oneg Shabbat' [clandestine Jewish communal archives in the Warsaw Ghetto] and for being the most endangered because I hid the entire material. It would be a small thing to give my own head. I risk the head of my dear wife Gele Seckstein and my treasure, my little daughter, Margalit.

I don't want any gratitude, any monument, any praise. I want only a remembrance, so that my family, brother and sister abroad, may know what has become of my remains.

I want my wife to be remembered. Gele Seckstein, artist, dozens of works, talented, didn't manage to exhibit, did not show in public. During the three years of war worked among children as educator, teacher, made stage sets, costumes for the children's productions, received awards. Now together with me, we are preparing to receive death.

I want my little daughter to be remembered. Margalit, 20 months old today. Has mastered Yiddish perfectly, speaks a pure Yiddish. At 9 months began to speak Yiddish clearly. In intelligence she is on a par with 3- or 4-year-old children. I don't want to brag about her. Witnesses to this, who tell me about it, are the teaching staff at the school . . .

I am not sorry about my life and that of my wife. But I am sorry for the gifted little girl. She deserves to be remembered also.

May we be the redeemers of all the rest of the Jews in the whole world. I believe in the survival of our people. Jews will not be annihilated. We, the Jews of Poland, Czechoslovakia, Lithuania, Latvia, are the scapegoats for all Israel in all the other lands.

July 31, 1942

Source: YIVO Archives, cited in Lucy Dawidowicz, A Holocaust Reader (Behrman House, 1976), pp. 296–97

The psychology of the victim **18**

When considering the behaviour of the victims, the Nobel Prize-winning writer, Elie Wiesel, himself a survivor of the camps, put it thus:

Reduced to a mere number, the man in the concentration camp at the same time lost his identity and his individual destiny. He came to realise that his presence in the camp was due solely to the fact that he was part of a forgotten and condemned collectivity. It is not written: I shall live or die, but: someone – today – will vanish, or will continue to suffer; and from the point of view of the collective, it makes no difference whether that someone is I or another. Only the number, only the quota counts. Thus, the one who had been spared, above all during the selections, could not repress his first spontaneous reflex of joy. A moment, a week, or an eternity later, this joy weighted with fear and anxiety will turn into guilt. 'I am happy to have escaped death' becomes equivalent to admitting: 'I am glad someone else went in my place.' It was in order not to think about this that the prisoners so very quickly managed to forget their comrades or their relatives: those who had been selected. They forgot them quickly – trying to shut their eyes to the reproachful glances which still floated in the air around them.

Why did the Jews in the camps not choose a death with honour, knife in hand and hate on their lips? It is understandable that all of us should wonder why. Putting aside the technical and psychological reasons which made any attempt at revolt impossible (the Jews knew they had been sacrificed, forgotten, crossed off by humanity), to answer we must consider the moral aspects of the question. The Jews, conscious of the curse weighing them down, came to believe that they were neither worthy nor capable of an act of honour. To die struggling would have meant a betrayal of those who had gone to their deaths submissive and silent. The only way was to follow in their footsteps, die their kind of death – only then could the living make their peace with those who had already gone.

I attended the Eichmann trial, I heard the prosecutor try to get the witnesses to talk by forcing them to expose themselves and to probe the innermost recesses of their being: why didn't you resist? Why didn't you attack your assassins when you outnumbered them?

Pale, embarrassed, ill at ease, the survivors all responded in the same way: 'You cannot understand. Anyone who wasn't there cannot imagine it.'

Well I was there. And I do not understand. I do not understand that child in the Warsaw Ghetto who wrote in his diary: 'I'm hungry, I'm cold; when I grow up I want to be a German, and then I won't be hungry any more.'

I still do not understand why I did not throw myself upon the Kapo, who was beating my father before my very eyes. In Galicia, Jews dug their own graves and lined up, without any trace of panic, at the edge of the trench to await the machine-gun barrage. I do not understand their calm. And that woman, that mother, in the bunker somewhere in Poland, I do not understand her either; her companions smothered her child for fear its cries might betray their presence; that woman, that mother, having lived this scene of biblical intensity, did not go mad. I do not understand her; why and by what right, and in the name of what, did she not go mad?

I do not know why, but I forbid us to ask the question.

Source: Elie Wiesel, Legends of Our Time *(Holt, Rinehart and Winston, 1968)*

19 Jewish disbelief at reports of mass annihilation

The following extract is taken from a report by Yitzhak Cukierman, a leader of the Pioneer Underground in occupied Poland and representative of the Jewish Fighting Organisation on the Aryan side in Warsaw. It was written in Warsaw in March 1944 and sent to London on 24 May 1944 via a courier for the Polish Underground.

The liquidation of the Jews in the General Government began at Passover 1942. The first victims were the Jews of the city of Lublin, and shortly after that the Jews of the whole District of Lublin. They were evacuated to Belzec, and there they were killed in new gas-chambers that had been built specially for this purpose. The Jewish Underground newspapers gave detailed descriptions of this mass slaughter. But [the Jews of] Warsaw did not believe it! Common human sense could not understand that it was possible to exterminate tens and hundreds of thousands of Jews. They decided that the Jews were being transported for agricultural work in the parts of Russia occupied by the Germans. Theories were heard that the Germans had begun on the productivisation of the Jewish lower-level bourgeoisie! The Jewish press was denounced and charged with causing panic, although the *descriptions* of the 'rooting out' of the population corresponded accurately to the reality. Not only abroad were the crimes of the Germans received with disbelief, but even here, close by Ponary, Chelmno, Belzec and Treblinka, did this information get no hearing! This unjustified optimism developed together with the lack of information, which was the result of total isolation from the outside world and the experience of the past. Had not the Germans for two and a half years carried out many deportations of Jews – from Cracow, from Lublin, from the Warsaw district and from the 'Reich'? Certainly there had been not a few victims and blood had been shed during these deportations, but total extermination?

There were some people who believed it, however. The events at Ponary and Chelmno were a fact, but – it was said – 'that was just a capricious act of the local authorities'. For, after all, the German authorities in the General Government did not have the same attitude to the ghettos in the cities and the small towns, not until death brought an equal fate to all. More than once, in various places, the reaction to the information we had about the liquidation of the Jews was: 'That cannot happen to us here.'

It was of course the Germans themselves who created these optimistic attitudes. Through two and a half years they prepared the work of exterminating the three and a half million Jews of Poland with German thoroughness. They rendered the Jewish masses helpless with the aid of ghettos and deportations. In years of unceasing experiments the Germans perfected their extermination methods. In Vilna they had needed several days to murder a thousand Jews, in Chelmno half an hour was enough to kill a hundred, and at Treblinka ten thousand were murdered every day.

Source: Yitzhak Arad, Yisrael Gutman and Abraham Margaliot (eds),
Documents on the Holocaust: Selected Sources on the Destruction of the
Jews of Germany and Austria, Poland, and the Soviet Union *(Yad Vashem Publications, 1981), Document 127*

PART III

GENOCIDE IN THE MODERN ERA

FINLAND
11

NORWAY
728

ESTONIA
1,000

North
Sea

LATVIA
80,000

Baltic Sea

MEMEL
8,000

LITHUANIA
135,000

WHITE
RUSSIA

WESTERN
RUSSIA

furthest German advance 1942

DENMARK
77

HOLLAND
106,000

BELGIUM
24,387

FREE CITY
OF DANZIG
1,000

GERMANY
160,000

POLAND
3,000,000

SOVIET
UNION
1,000,000

VOLHYNIA

LUXEMBOURG
700

CZECHOSLOVAKIA
217,000

RUTHENIA
60,000

GALICIA

PODOLIA

UKRAINE

BUKOVINA
124,632

BESSARABIA
200,000

AUSTRIA
65,000

NORTHERN
TRANSYLVANIA
105,000

FRANCE
83,000

HUNGARY
200,000

CRIMEA

RUMANIA
40,000

Black
Sea

ITALY

Adriatic Sea

YUGOSLAVIA
60,000

8,000

7,122
4,221

MACE-
DONIA

THRACE

Aegean Sea

ALBANIA
200

GREECE
65,000

KOS
120

RHODES
1,700

CRETE
260

Mediterranean
Sea

LIBYA
562

miles   300
0

0   kilometres   400

Frontiers (Northern Transylvania,
of 1937   in 1940)

© Martin Gilbert 1982

4   Jews murdered between 1 September 1939 and 8 May 1945: An estimate

> Genghis Khan had millions of women and men killed by his
> own will and with a gay heart. History sees in him only a great
> state builder . . . I have sent to the east . . . my 'Death's Head
> Units', with the order to kill without mercy men, women and
> children of Polish race or language. Only in such a way will
> we win the 'lebensraum' that we need. Who, after all, talks
> nowadays of the extermination of the Armenians?
>
> Adolf Hitler, 1939[1]

Many commentators have attempted to define the Nazi Holocaust by
relating it to the crime of 'genocide' – a rather loose term generally denoting
the destruction, or attempted destruction, of the whole or part of an
identifiable human group. The Holocaust has been variously described as
the 'ultimate genocide'; as an unparalleled crime that is 'beyond genocide';
and, on occasions, as simply 'another genocide'. Without denying the unique
and distinctive features of each and every such man-made catastrophe, it is
helpful – though decidedly depressing – to consider the Holocaust against
the background of other instances of genocide, both alleged and undisputed.

A question of definition?

Genocide is surely nothing new. The Bible is replete with apparent examples,
as are the chronicles of the ancient and classical worlds. The causes may
vary – wave upon wave of human migration, nomadic peoples pitted against
settled agricultural societies, 'advanced' civilizations versus loose-knit tribal
groupings, struggles for limited or decreasing natural resources – but the
genocidal pattern has been both long-term and unmistakable. The displacement and destruction of one human group by another, and the consequent
obliteration of cultures and societies into the sands of time, is a significant
aspect of our recorded history which we ignore at our peril.

Yet the term 'genocide' is new. It was the Nazi persecution and eventual
extermination of European Jewry in the 1940s that prompted Raphael
Lemkin, a prominent international lawyer, to propose it. ('Genos' is the
Greek for race or tribe, 'cide' from the Latin for killing.)[2] Lemkin's purpose
was to bring attention not merely to cases involving the actual destruction
of national or religious groups but also to the potential for such actions. In
an international community, he believed, such crimes against humanity
ought to be outlawed and punishable.

Significantly, after the Second World War, Lemkin's proposals found an
international legal context. In 1946, the newly formed United Nations, still
reeling from the horrors perpetrated on civilian communities in Nazi
Europe, moved to adopt a Genocide Convention. The General Assembly
appointed a committee to study the issue and make proposals on how the
Convention could best be formulated. At the outset, it sought to further
define the problem. Genocide, the committee stated, entailed: 'deliberate
acts committed with the intent to destroy a national, racial, religious or

political group on grounds of the national or racial origin, religious belief or political opinion of its members'.

Although this broad definition was not adopted in the actual Genocide Convention of 1948, the final text was, theoretically, a breakthrough in that it made genocide, or its intent, a punishable crime. So too were the powers, though somewhat ill-defined, which the United Nations gave to itself to prevent or suppress it. On the other hand, a number of commentators have noted the exclusion both of political and economic groups, and of 'minorities' (national, cultural, or religious) from its express protection – an omission which, it has been argued, appeared to come very close to giving member-state signatories a licence to commit the very act which the Convention set out to outlaw.[3]

In addition, the Convention was weakened by a number of member-states which insisted on emasculating its terms of reference. Prominent in this respect was the Soviet Union, which asserted that genocide, as committed by the Nazis, was bound up with a decaying phase of imperialism, the implication being that the Convention would be unlikely to have any future application. Perhaps it was felt that a full definition, enshrined in international law, would in some way encroach upon and threaten the sovereignty of independent states – the very bodies most capable of committing the crime in question. What is quite beyond dispute, however, is that, despite the adoption of this Convention by the United Nations, genocide has continued to disfigure human existence on this planet.

Article II of the United Nations Genocide Convention of 1948 eventually contained the following definition:

> genocide means any of the following acts committed with intent to destroy, in whole or in part, a national, ethnical, racial or religious group, as such:
>
> a) killing members of the group;
> b) causing serious bodily or mental harm to members of the group;
> c) deliberately inflicting on the group conditions of life calculated to bring about its physical destruction in whole or in part;
> d) imposing measures intending to prevent births within the group;
> e) forcibly transferring children of the group to another group.

Key questions remain unresolved. In the light of the savagery of human history, in what ways, if any, can genocide be considered a modern phenomenon? To what extent is it, in the final analysis, principally a question of numbers? To be sure, the technology of destruction, the sheer firepower alone, has in our century led to violent death on an unprecedented scale. Sociologists sometimes talk of twentieth-century 'mega-deaths'. But that in itself begs a series of questions. Are all mega-deaths cases of genocide? Alternatively, where the numbers involved are relatively small, can this not also constitute genocide? When exactly do we cross the border? When does inter-communal massacre (e.g. in the Lebanon or Sri Lanka) become genocide? At what point does violence against individuals or collections of individuals, man-induced hunger, torture and murder, become a cumulative act called genocide? To what extent can the 'ethnic cleansing' of regions, especially characteristic of the recent conflict in the former Yugoslavia, be accurately described as genocide? To be more specific, do these acts have features in common? Is it possible to link (compare?) the main subject of this book – the extermination of the Jews during the Second World War – to other mass killings?[4]

The nine case studies below – one nineteenth-century example and the rest from the twentieth century – suggest that there may well be some common characteristics associated with both the causes and implementation of genocide. This is not to say that the purpose here is to establish a simple theory or model of genocide. The case studies, moreover, are not intended as a comprehensive or up-to-date list. There are at least three times as many twentieth-century cases – the vast majority occurring *since* the Nazi horrors – that might arguably have been included. Nor are they intended to propose a pecking order. A number of the most quantitatively severe cases are not included, while one or two that have taken relatively few lives are. The aim of the exercise is not to prove that one genocide was more horrible, or worse, than another. For the human beings involved, whichever act it was and whatever term may be used to describe it, the experience was total and final.

However, these case studies do propose to demonstrate, in spite of the diverse contexts in which they take place, that acts of genocide (and massacre) are not exclusive to any one human group. They are indeed a universal phenomenon. They can be committed by white against black and vice versa, black against black, white against white, right against left and vice versa, majorities against minorities and vice versa. What is more, the victims can, when the context is changed, become the perpetrators.

This does not mean, however, that genocide cannot be categorized in some way. For instance, one observer (Helen Fein) has suggested the following categories,[5] to which I have tentatively assigned some noted twentieth-century cases – often referred to as genocides, though not always undisputedly so.

Ideological genocides Committed with the aim of promoting a particular doctrine or ideology:

- Turks against Armenians, 1915
- Soviet communist destruction of Kulaks, 1929–32
- Nazi Holocaust but also mass killings of Byelo-Russians, Poles, Gypsies and Ukrainians, 1941–45
- Khmer Rouge versus Cambodian people, 1975–79

Retributive genocides Punitive murderous policy to ensure, or restore, the domination of one ethnic group or class within a state against the threat by a subordinate class or ethnic group:

- Nazi-backed Croats versus Serbs, 1941
- French in Algeria (then part of metropolitan France), 1945–62
- Sudanese government against black Christian southern Sudanese, 1955–92
- post-Sukarno regime versus Indonesian Communists, 1965–67
- Nigerian army versus Ibos (Biafra), 1966–70
- Pakistani military against Bengalis, 1971
- Tutsi against Hutu of Burundi (Africa), 1972
- Pinochet regime in Chile, 1973
- Guatemalan military against Mayan Indians, 1980–present
- Ethiopian regime against peoples of Tigray and Eritrea, 1980–92
- Iraqi government versus Kurds, 1988 and 1991 and against Marsh Arabs, 1991–present

Developmental genocides Committed with the aim of eliminating an indigenous population, usually outside of the political structure, which is deemed to stand in the way of colonization, settlement or development:

- Germans against Herreros of South West Africa, 1905
- Pakistan (later Bangladesh) against Chittagong Hill Tract tribes, late 1940s–present
- Brazilian and Paraguayan governments against Ache and other Amerindians, 1960s–present
- Communist China against Tibet, 1959–present
- Indonesia against West Papua and East Timor, 1969 and 1975 respectively–present

Despotic genocides Committed with the purpose of demonstrating and/or consolidating power by the use of force against both potential opponents and the population at large:

- Stalin against Soviet party and selected elements of population, 1936–53
- Macias government of Equatorial Guinea 1968–79
- Amin government and successors against Ugandans (especially Ugandan Asians), 1972–85
- Argentinian junta versus the political 'left', 1978–79 (including the period of the Soccer World Cup, staged during the summer of 1978 in Argentina, on which the eyes of much of the world were consequently focused!)

Such categorization is neither complete nor precise. It excludes cases of foreign powers engaged in war, notably United States forces in Vietnam

(1960s–1973) and Soviet forces in Afghanistan (1979–89), both of whom were accused of genocidal war crimes against the native populations. Moreover, in practice the above terms of reference may on occasions overlap so much as to make them almost meaningless. To take just one example, the destruction of the Armenians was certainly ideological. However, it could also quite validly be construed as a developmental genocide, given that the Ottoman authorities unquestionably wanted to consolidate their pan-Turkic empire, (implying colonization of non-Turkic districts), while Turkish justification (though not admission of the act of genocide) has always revolved around the Armenian 'threat' to the Ottoman body politic. This would place their response in both the 'retributive' or 'despotic' categories, too.[6]

Conditions for genocide

Genocide is perpetrated in particular circumstances and in particular human and social environments. One factor having an inevitable bearing on the outcome is the historical context. Thus, one hundred or two hundred years ago the agent of genocide might have been a colonial power removing a defiant or ungovernable indigenous population from its path. Today, the more likely agent will be its post-decolonization successor attempting to 'pacify' or remove its own unintegrated or assimilating minorities. That, of course, is not to presume that all colonization or decolonization will lead to genocide. This is clearly not the case. A society may have genocidal potential without ever perpetrating – or even contemplating – the act. Northern Ireland, for instance, has a history of settlement reflecting the colonizing power of Britain. Centuries ago the Protestant newcomers from the British mainland displaced or marginalized the religiously and culturally quite distinct indigenous community and after the independence of the south (Eire), in 1921, continued to exclude the Catholic minority from political and economic power. Given that across the border in Eire, the majority population was Catholic, the potential for a genocidal explosion did, and arguably continues to, exist. In 1969, a civil disaster seemed imminent but was forestalled by the arrival of British troops. Sectarian strife, of course, remains unrelenting and is punctuated by outbursts of murder and atrocities. Both the Protestant majority and the Catholic minority continue to perceive themselves as threatened. But the outcome, to date, has not been genocidal.[7]

Nor, interestingly, did the predicament in South Africa prove genocidal. This provides us with a paradox. The apartheid regime was a classic example of a minority settler population, whose domination of the majority was crudely, though effectively, founded on a system of racial hierarchy and exclusiveness. This domination was upheld through both law and brute force, the latter being most particularly deployed at key moments in the early 1960s and late 1970s, when the system came under serious challenge. But,

although these situations again clearly had genocidal potential, two important factors held them in check. First, apartheid society was economically
dependent on the black majority for its labour force. Exemplary killings and
terror might have been of assistance in cowing the majority population, but
to destroy it altogether would – to put it mildly – have been counter-
productive. Secondly, the ruling white minority continued to perceive itself
as somehow functioning within the cultural and moral framework, and
certainly under the scrutiny, of white European Christian 'civilization' and, as
such, was still subject to behavioural constraints.

Subjugation of a group is clearly not the same as elimination, although the
borderline separating the two may be tenuous. We may consider, as a related
example, the Spanish and Portuguese imperial conquests of Central and
South America, from the sixteenth to the eighteenth century. The impact
of these events on the indigenous society was catastrophic and irreversible,
a total population of perhaps 40 million in 1492 collapsing to no more than
18 million by 1800, with hundreds of communities and cultures eradicated.
Yet there seems to have been no exterminatory blueprint. Enslavement,
yes; obliteration of a native political and cultural life (which might, in its
effects, be tantamount to genocide), yes; physical extermination, no. Mass
destruction was as important a feature of what happened here as in North
America (where a stronger case could be made for colonial genocide
having taken place), yet most of the evidence points to the transmission of
the old world's infectious diseases (particularly smallpox, measles, influenza
and typhus) and the introduction of bacteria – harmless to Europeans but
to which the local population had developed no immunity – as the primary
cause of large-scale fatalities.

Ironically, though, as the whole imperial enterprise was based on the social
subjugation and economic exploitation of the indigenous population, these
demographic losses had to be made good elsewhere. Enslaved black Africans,
transported in their millions across the Atlantic, provided the answer. And
between 1.2 million and 2.6 million, in the three main centuries of the trade,
are estimated to have died in the process. Again the figures suggest genocide.
The context, however, despite the implicit brutality and viciousness of the
circumstances, does not. Slaves were chattels to be bought and sold and were
thus only of value alive. It was pathogens not policy that killed so many of
them, as, in relative terms, it did to similar numbers of their European
captors. Genocidal intent, in this instance, may be ruled out.

In terms of human misery, of course, our exclusion of particular examples
from the various categories of genocide, may seem not only tasteless and
inappropriate but ultimately futile. All surely are encompassed under a more
general heading which we might call 'crimes against humanity'. Our purpose,
however, is to show that genocide is a particular type of crime, occurring in
special circumstances but not in others.

One last grey area may illustrate this point. In the multi-ethnic, multireligious Lebanon, from the mid-1970s to the late-1980s inter-communal violence spilled over into examples of what some observers described as genocidal massacre. For those caught in the eye of this storm, arguments about the precise definition of genocide are again irrelevant. In terms of a broad overview, however, systematic genocide did not take place. The will to commit it may well have been there. The Christian Phalange, its Maronite Christian rivals, the fundamentalist Islamic Hizbollah and sections of the Palestinian and Druze militias may all, at given moments, have wished their immediate neighbours removed from the face of the earth. Yet, despite the ever-mounting death toll, this did not happen. Genocide might well have occurred if any one group or alliance of groups had been able to dominate the scene. This threat came perilously close during the Israeli invasion of the highly fragmented state [of Lebanon] in 1982, which seemed – unintentionally – to provide a cover for its Phalangist allies to contemplate and partially undertake a genocidal action against the Palestinians. Since then, however, the ensuing military and political stalemate between the various militias and their respective Iraqi, Syrian, Iranian or Israeli allies, while on the one hand ensuring the continuing threat of violent conflict and bloodshed, on the other may paradoxically have offered the only restraint on unbridled genocide.[8]

Genocide in action

What gives genocide its distinctive characteristics is both the motivation and the ability to carry it out. The potential victims have to be collectively defined, selected, isolated from non-victims, and then obliterated. It is a process that is both deliberate and systematic. If it cannot be carried out all at once, then it is something to which the perpetrators will wish to return. On the other hand, they must be sure that they will be ultimately success-ful. To do less may be to suffer retribution at the hands of the victims or of some other, more powerful, external agent. Indeed, the true 'state of the art' is the genocide where the act has been so complete, the incriminating evidence so utterly disposed of, that the perpetrators can deny that it ever happened.

Only one body in modern society can consider such an undertaking with seriousness and equanimity: the state. Only the state is fully equipped with the necessary apparatus for the task; the technology of destruction, the logistical and administrative support systems, the communications facilities with which to coordinate its campaign and the 'disinformation' agencies with which to lie to its wider population and to the world at large.

Needless to say, this does not mean that many states spend their time contemplating, let alone perpetrating, genocide. Tolerant or fully homo-geneous states will not, of course, ever consider it. Even states that, by the volatile nature of their multi-racial and multi-national composition, have genocidal potential will in all probability never have recourse to it. Relations between dominant and subordinate ethnic or sectarian groups, between religious and national majorities and minorities, between the settled agricultural or urban populations and the hunter-gatherers or nomads on society's fringe may simply subsist. Friction may be endemic; there may be a syndrome of 'us' and 'them', possibly even a virulent view of a particular group or groups as outsiders, strangers or pariahs, which is reflected in episodes of spontaneous or random killings. Certainly these relations represent potential preconditions for genocide. They do not, however, determine or explain its implementation.

Genocide, in other words, needs an additional ingredient – a *catalyst*, some extraordinary event or development which will transform a 'normal' situation into a truly genocidal one. It may be that the catalyst is external to both perpetrators and victims, perhaps an economic crisis, drought, famine or some other disaster, which has the effect of bringing dormant tensions to the surface in what may end up as a frenzied explosion of violence against the appointed scapegoat group. But even this near spontaneous outburst of pogrom and atrocity is likely to fall short of pre-meditated annihilation. The protagonists in such events may be groups of highly motivated or, perhaps, only temporarily inflamed individuals, carried away by the dynamics of mob rule. To be transformed into true genocide, however, the state itself must be the protagonist.

And here we come to the heart and essence of the urge to genocide. Why would a state act in such a way against any group either within or outside of its political sphere of influence? The answer in short is this: the state would have to be convinced, very convinced, that this extraordinary crisis could only be resolved by exterminating its selected victim group. That would mean that the victim group would have to be perceived not simply as a grave but, indeed, as a mortal threat to the state itself. The reasoning might go something like this: 'If we do not destroy them, they will destroy us. Our action therefore is no ordinary one and cannot be limited by moral or legal restraints. On the contrary, because "they" are the enemy, a veritable cancer threatening our very existence, our sanction to act, as we propose, is absolute; our mission is "sacred".'

By such a process, therefore, the will to genocide becomes elevated to the 'highest' plane, indeed to a pseudo-religious duty. The corollary is that the victim group must be degraded to the level of 'ein mistvolk', Adolf Eichmann's term for what he perceived as a garbage nation 'fit only for the dung heap'. This dehumanization, this negation not simply of the victims' human attributes but of their very right to exist, is the necessary prelude to an important aspect of genocide's agenda: not merely the annihilation of the group but its obliteration from the state and wider historical record.[9]

Even in crises and exceptional circumstances, one would assume, however, that most states would fall short of this all-embracing response. The record of the twentieth century nevertheless shows us that where the state machinery is controlled or has been captured by a highly motivated group or party with its own very definite ideas about the nature and organization of that society, it has sometimes not shrunk from genocidal intent and action. This is perhaps the final clue and warning signal as to the nature of genocide. Genocide may occur where normal societal restraints have been removed or frozen. More specifically, it happens during or, more often, in the wake of war, revolution or some other massive political dislocation, such as decolonization. In the most complete examples, it is carried out by an ideologically motivated clique, with its own particular sense of destiny, which, having consolidated state control, is able to act against the victim group with seeming impunity. For this purpose it will require either the active participation of the wider population, their acquiescence or, failing that, their neutralization. Genocide is the response, almost always, of a totalitarian society, in which dissent or doubt are themselves crimes.

That it is the state (or the agents of the state) that is the perpetrator of genocide tells us one other revealing fact. Other states will not intervene unless their own state interests are threatened. They may be appalled bystanders but they will remain bystanders none the less. One of the hallmarks of genocide, demonstrated with the utmost poignancy in the recent case of Bosnia, has been the international community's inaction until it is too late. In this sense, the United Nations Genocide Convention has in practice been a dead letter.[10]

Case studies[11]

1 Tasmanian Aborigines, 1803–36

Place   Tasmania, southern island off Australia, separated from mainland by Bass Strait.

Estimated deaths   No precise figures exist but the native population of between 3,000 and 5,000 natives was completely wiped out.

Immediate catalyst   Last-ditch efforts by indigenous population to defend their native hunting grounds.

Context   Colonization of Australian continent by British.

Background   Though explorers like Tasman and Cook visited Van Dieman's land (later called Tasmania) in the seventeenth and eighteenth centuries and, in the latter case, had remarked on the gentle bearing of its hunter-gatherer inhabitants, there was no European attempt to colonize the island until 1803. Its aboriginal peoples, believed to be of a stock quite different from those on the other side of Bass Strait, had lived unmolested in its dense rain forests for some 30,000 years. Abundant kangaroo were an important and integral part of their diet and culture. The arrival of British penal colonies, however, posed a direct and potentially fatal threat to this existence. Initially, before they became agriculturally self-sufficient, the colonists competed for and almost eradicated the kangaroo. Almost as a by-product, atrocities against the natives quickly became a feature of an illegal bushranger society which developed beyond the long arm of the govern-ment settlements. More serious was the accelerating rate of colonization and development. By 1824, there were more than 12,000 white inhabitants, mostly convicts, involved in slave labour, logging, sheep-stock raising and the building of a north–south trunk road. By this time, the governance of the island was in the hands of Sir George Arthur, who has been credited with the creation of a system that was the nearest thing the British empire ever had to a totalitarian police society. Although Arthur, under the auspices of his Committee for Aboriginal Affairs, superficially appeared to be pursuing a policy that aimed at the protection of the natives, in reality he developed a system that encouraged convicts to track and capture them as one way of working their freedom. Increasingly desperate, the natives fought back, killing sheep and settlers and provoking hysterical demands from the white population that Arthur solve the 'black problem'.

Nature of genocide Entrapment, poisoning and torture of the natives had been a haphazard feature of the 'black wars' for a number of years. Arthur's action in 1830, however, was systematic, in that it placed the settled part of the island under martial law as a prelude to an organized manhunt, designed to remove all the 'blacks' from that region. Practically the whole white male population participated in this operation, involving two great lines of beaters moving across the island in an 'immense pheasant-drive'. Though, in fact, only a handful of natives were captured or killed, the remainder were driven into coastal pockets and peninsulas, where they were eventually cajoled into captivity by an expedition – assisted by 'tamed' abo-rigines – that promised food and safe haven. For the few hundred survivors this turned out to be concentration on Flinders Island in Bass Strait. There, despite efforts to Europeanize them, they died of despair, demoralization, smallpox and tuberculosis.

World response Observers like Charles Darwin, who at the time happened to be in Hobart harbour on HMS *Beagle*, were appalled. Outrage was also expressed by a few liberals and humanitarians in Britain. Otherwise, there was no response.

Perpetrators' defence The colonial administrators blamed the natives themselves for committing 'unprovoked acts of barbarity' and claimed that they, in response, were only 'defending their interests'. A more general view of the settlers was that the aborigines were unreformable, lazy savages who, given that they did not till the earth like 'Christian' folk, had forfeited their right to it.

Long-term results   Like the unique Tasmanian Devil Cat, which was hunted to extinction, and the breeding colonies of right whales, which were annihilated in the Derwent river estuary, so too the native people of Tasmania became casualties of the white man's invasion and consolidation. The population was reduced to 50 individuals within seven years of their removal to Flinders Island and the last pure-blooded native died in 1876.

2 Armenians, 1915–16

Place   Mostly Armenian provinces of Ottoman Empire. Modern-day Eastern Turkey.

Estimated deaths   1.5 million.

Immediate catalyst   First World War Turkish disasters on Russian Caucasus front.

Context   Great Power rivalries and emerging national movements in declining years of Ottoman empire.

Background   The Armenians are a distinct ethnic, religious and linguistic group, with their own Orthodox Christian Church and history of nation-hood dating back at least to Roman times. The Armenian homeland, however, centred on Lake Van, had been politically absorbed by successive Muslim empires since the eleventh century. Under the millet system of the Ottoman Turks, the Armenians were able to maintain their religious and jurisdictional autonomy, played key commercial and bureaucratic roles in the empire and developed a widespread diaspora. This essentially tolerant situation came under increasing strain in the mid- and late nineteenth century. The Ottoman's northern rival, Tsarist Russia, assisted Rumanian, Bulgarian, Serb and other Balkan groups who wanted to break away from the empire, while pursuing its own policy of expansion at the Ottomans' expense. Parts of Armenia fell into Russian hands, stimulating an emerging Armenian national movement to hope that it, too, like the Balkan provinces, would be able to create its own state, possibly under Russian protection. In the period 1894–96, the Turkish Sultan responded to a localized Armenian revolution-ary rising with genocidal massacres of some 300,000 Armenians. In 1908, however, the 'Young Turk' movement toppled the autocratic Sultan in a coup and set up a new regime committed to modernization and the Turkization of the empire, including Armenia. In 1914, it entered the war on the side of Germany and the Central Powers, hoping to create an expanded Pan-Turkic empire. The great majority of Turkish Armenian leaders offered loyalty, or at least acquiescence, in the empire's war against Russia, and Armenian conscripts into the Turkish forces were prominent in the war effort. Enver Pasha and the other Young Turk leaders, however, perceived them collectively both as a group that stood in the way of these Turkish aspirations and as potential fifth columnists who would offer assistance to the Russians.

Nature of genocide Following the Turkish defeat against the Russians at Sarikamish in late 1914, Young Turk policy towards the Armenians underwent a fundamental change, leading to a stage-by-stage but calculated process culminating in genocide. Battalions of Armenian soldiers were converted into slave labour squads and later systematically shot. In April 1915, able-bodied men in villages and towns throughout the empire were rounded up, imprisoned and again usually executed. Within the next few months, women, the old, the young and the sick were sometimes also executed *en masse* but more often were herded into forced marches towards the Turkish interior and Syrian desert – an almost unbelievable caravan of human misery. There they died in their hundreds of thousands, through a combination of brutality, starvation, cold and disease. This process was not systematic in the sense that all people were massacred in the same way or at the same place, but seems to have been left to the local initiative of the gendarmerie and the Young Turks' own special para-military organization, the Teshkilat-i Makhsusiye. As with the 1895 massacres, Kurdish tribesmen were often active auxiliaries in the process. There was also some armed, but ultimately ineffectual, resistance on the part of the Armenian victims. The cumulative effect was the removal and liquidation of Armenians from the provinces where they formed a majority and from Turkish society in general.

World response The events in Armenia were known both to Henry Morgenthau, the US ambassador in Constaninople, and to German and Austrian diplomats. Appeals were made to Enver Pasha but to no effect. Indeed, they were deemed counter-productive. There were accurate media reports of the atrocities on both sides in the war. The Allies charged that the Turkish leadership would be held responsible and promised the establishment of an Armenian state at the end of the war. Although Armenians themselves attempted to set up this state in 1918, assistance from the Allies failed to materialize, since international calculations – associated with the emergence of a new, independent Turkey under Mustafa Kemal – now took precedence.

Perpetrators' defence The Turks, both at the diplomatic level and in academic works, have gone to strenuous lengths over the past seventy-five years consistently to deny that any such genocide took place. They have argued, first, that the Armenians had constituted a threat to the Turkish homeland, had sided with the Russians in the war and had fomented rebellion (i.e. by implication they deserved what they had got), and, secondly, that what have been referred to as 'deportations' were in fact 'relocations', put into effect for the Armenians' own protection (i.e. no massacres had taken place or where they had happened were 'isolated incidents' perpetrated by renegades and bandits).

Long-term results During the period 1918–23, the new Turkey consolidated its grip on all of the former Armenian provinces of the Ottoman empire and also added parts of the Armenian homeland that had previously been under Tsarist Russian control. These developments were accompanied by further massacres of Armenians, especially during the short-lived Turkish occupation of the Caspian sea port of Baku. The Armenian republic, encompassing only one tenth of what was formerly Armenian territory and with half a million refugees from Turkey, survived by accepting Russian Bolshevik tutelage. Parts of it, notably Nagorno-Karabakh, were awarded to the neighbouring Turkic-speaking Soviet republic of Azerbaijan which, in the late 1980s, with the decline of central Soviet power, has led to renewed Armenian fears of genocidal massacre. The 1915 genocide remains central to the Armenian experience in both Armenia itself and the world-wide Armenian diaspora. In recent years, there has been a renewed spate of assassinations of Turkish diplomats around the world by Armenian nationalists seeking to avenge the events of 1915.

3 Kulaks,[12] 1929–33

Place Specifically the Ukraine and other non-Russian regions within the Soviet Union.

Estimated deaths Conservative estimates range between 11 and 14.5 million.

Immediate catalyst Crash programme of collectivization of Soviet agriculture.

Context Post-revolutionary phase of Communist Party programme to impose its ideology and practice on Soviet society.

Background When the Bolshevik Party under Lenin seized power in

November 1917, it did so in the full expectation that its example, through emulation in the more industrialized countries of the west, would lead to a world revolution. However, when these developments were either arrested or failed to materialize, Marxist-Leninism was faced with the problem of how to create 'socialism in one country'. The party's blueprint for this task involved the transformation of an overwhelmingly peasant society into a modern industrial nation. However, because the communist ideology behind this transformation was opposed by the majority of the population, it followed that the Bolsheviks' programme could only be achieved through coercion.

In the period of the civil war between 1918 and 1921, the Bolsheviks had attempted to impose control on the countryside by a system of 'war communism', requisitioning grain surpluses from peasant communes. This had led, amongst other things, to both famine and widespread peasant rebellions and became the critical factor in Lenin's change of course, in 1921, towards a limited free-market economy. The New Economic Policy may have given the peasantry a few years' respite, but Communist Party ideology remained the same. The countryside would ultimately have to be harnessed to a communized industrial system through 'collectivization'. In short, this required the peasant to become an agricultural worker on a state-organized farm, while those who stood in the way of the process, characterized as 'kulaks', would be eliminated. No satisfactory communist definition existed as to who in practice constituted these 'class enemies'. Nevertheless, with the rise of Stalin within the party, and with what appeared to be another grain short-fall in the countryside, in 1929 the party apparatus committed itself to a five year plan aimed simultaneously at the systematic elimination of the kulaks ('dekulakization') and at collectivization of the countryside. The focus of this operation was the Ukraine, the traditional 'grain basket' of the old empire and a region that, in the civil war, had attempted – unsuccessfully – to form a sovereign state. Under Soviet hegemony, by 1929 it still retained some vestiges of a national and cultural independence.

Nature of genocide   Secret police squads (OGPU, a forerunner of the KGB) and party activists were sent into the countryside to requisition grain, dispossess peasants of their private holdings and concentrate them in state 'collective' farms. Millions of small landowners and their families were imprisoned, shot or deported to slave labour camps in northern Siberia and the Arctic circle, where most were starved or worked to death. Peasant resistance, primarily through the slaughter of livestock, put a check to the wholesale implementation of collectivization. The party responded, however, in 1931–32, by confiscating all remaining food and by raising grain quotas, particularly in the Ukraine. This resulted in a man-made famine of epidemic proportions. Available grain stocks were denied to the peasants, while the conscious and methodical blocking by OGPU troops of exits from the famine zone led to the slow and painful annihilation of some 6 million peasants. This was in addition to a similar figure already eliminated through 'dekulakization'. Simultaneously, the Ukrainian intellectual and political élite – including the majority of the republic's party apparatus – was purged and liquidated.

World response Despite the USSR's isolation from the world, there was accurate media coverage of the famine in the western press, though this was offset by articles and avowedly eyewitness accounts from Soviet sympathizers that denied its existence. In the midst of world depression, most countries had problems of their own and were therefore extremely reluctant to take action. Some, like the USA, had no diplomatic relationship with the Soviet Union. Moreover, recent intervention by western powers in the Russian civil war had, it was agreed, proved costly, dubious and ultimately disastrous, and seemed as good a reason as any for keeping a safe distance from the Soviet Union's current internal difficulties.

Perpetrators' defence The Soviet Union officially took two lines. First, though it did not deny 'dekulakization' or collectivization, it refused to admit that this had been genocidal in character. Nor, it was asserted, had there had been any famine. Secondly, while conceding that there had been some food shortages, it claimed this was due to natural causes or to sabotage by kulaks and other 'class enemies'.

Long-term results The events of 1929–32 can be viewed as part of a wider pattern of genocidal activity, perpetrated under Stalin, against national and ethnic groups, as well as against perceived political opponents, mostly from within the Communist Party ranks. This resulted in the deaths of no fewer than 20 million people (excluding deaths from the Second World War). In the western Ukraine, for instance, seized by the Soviets from Poland in 1939 and then 'liberated' again from the Nazis in 1944, a similar process – elimination of the country's political and intellectual leadership – took place to that which had occurred in the eastern Ukraine in the early 1930s. The strength of national and regional opposition to Soviet control had not been destroyed, however, as was reflected in the Ukrainian and other national movements that arose during Gorbachev's 'reconstruction'. As for the Soviet government itself, under Khrushchev's leadership, Stalin's mass party purges in the period 1936–41 were denounced, though not the earlier and more extensive genocide of 1929–32. The Gorbachev regime, which marked the transition from communism to the post-communist break-up of much of the multi-national Soviet empire – in contrast and perhaps somewhat ambivalently – acknowledged the scope, scale and responsibility of its predecessors' actions.

4 Roma (Gypsies), 1941–45

Place Germany and Nazi-occupied Europe.

Estimated deaths 250,000.

Immediate catalyst Full-blown implementation of Nazi racial ideology following invasion of the Soviet Union.

Context Nazi racial and ideological war of extermination against Jews and accompanying subjugation of '*untermenschen*' (subhumanity) in occupied Europe during the Second World War.

Background The Roma's origins are as a distinct ethnic and linguistic group dating back to great migrations from the Indian sub-continent beginning some 1,500 years ago. Present almost everywhere throughout the European continent, possessing strong family and clan ties and with a social and economic culture based on migration, they have become outsiders par excellence. As such, Gypsies, as they are known to settled societies, have been the constant focus of prejudice, legal discrimination and persecution. The Nazis thus inherited a traditional and well-embedded view of Gypsies as an anti-social (or asocial) class, closely associated with criminality. In addition, they were inclined to view Gypsies alongside other ethnic, particularly East European Slavic, peoples as inferiors – '*untermenschen*' – and classified them accordingly. There was, however, a paradox in this thinking. They distinguished between 'pure' Roma who were perceived to be 'Aryan' and impure Gypsy 'non-Ayrans'. Consequently – and amazingly – while some Roma were being butchered at Auschwitz, others were serving in the German army. Indeed Himmler, the Head of the SS, is said personally to have intervened to exempt the perceived 'Aryan' variety from the exterminatory process.

Nature of genocide While the peculiarities, or possibly confusion, of Nazi attitudes to Roma provided some loopholes for survival not available to Jews, the system of annihilation of Gypsies has close parallels with the 'Final Solution' of the Jewish question. German Gypsies were among those used for '*sonderbehandlung*': special treatment in gassing experiments between January 1940 and August 1941. Gypsies too were rounded up for 'resettlement' in all the countries occupied by the Nazis and deported east to ghettos and to labour, concentration and extermination camps, often adjacent to, but separate from, their Jewish inmates. Round-ups, summary executions as well as disease – particularly typhus – all took a massive toll. During the Nazi invasion of the Soviet Union, Gypsies were killed by SS death squads (*Einsaztgruppen*) when they were caught; they were also murdered elsewhere, particularly by the fascist Ustasi or Nyilas groups in Croatia and later in Hungary alongside Serbs, Jews, communists and other 'undesirables'. They were among the first to be exterminated in the experimental gassing units at Chelmno in early 1942. Most commentators agree that Gypsies sent to the special Gypsy Camp (*Zigeunerlage*) at Auschwitz-Birkenau or other death camps were not destined for total extermination, as was the case with Jews. Nevertheless, thousands of Gypsies died in medical experiments in the camps and thousands more in the gas chambers of Majdanek, Sobibor, Belzec, Treblinka, Auschwitz-Birkenau and elsewhere. In all, it is estimated that nearly a quarter of Roma's population in Nazi-occupied Europe was annihilated.

World response   No action was taken on behalf of Roma during the war, though the indictment of German war criminals at the Nuremberg tribunal in 1946 cited Gypsies, alongside Poles and Jews, as peoples who had been the victims of 'deliberate and systematic genocide'.

Perpetrators' defence   According to Nazi philosophy, Gypsies, in particular those perceived as 'non-Ayran' Gypsies, were a social and racial menace.

Long-term results   Unlike the Jewish encounter with Nazism, there is very little documentary or historical material dealing with the Nazis' onslaught against Europe's Gypsy population. This is perhaps part of the explanation why no compensation was ever paid by West Germany to Gypsy survivors, as was paid to Jewish survivor-victims. The same failure is true of companies that, under the Nazis, employed slave labour. This lamentable position shows gradual signs of improvement: there have in recent years been specific commemorations and a recognition by the West German government in 1982 that what happened to the Gypsies was indeed a crime of genocide. This has opened up the possibility of legal redress and financial reparation through the West German courts. Demographically, too, the position of European Roma is improving. They continue to be a widespread minority, especially in Eastern Europe, and in some countries have been recognized as a national group. On the other hand, the persistence of anti-Gypsy prejudice is a factor making for continued harassment and discrimination in many European societies.

5 *Bengalis, 1971*

Place   Bangladesh, formerly East Pakistan.

Estimated deaths   Between 1.25 and 3 million.

Immediate catalyst   The threatened break-up of Pakistan.

Context   Decolonization in the Indian sub-continent superseded by economic and political domination of one part of a successor state over another.

Background   The partition of British India, in 1947, into the successor states of India and Pakistan had been accompanied at the outset by sectarian massacres, perpetrated at a grass-roots level by both Hindus and Muslims. These were particularly extensive in the Bengal region which was itself divided between the two new states. The new Pakistan was nominally held together by Islam. However, complicating factors existed: its eastern Bengali wing was geographically separated from the west by 1,000 miles of India; both East and West Pakistan were highly diverse, culturally, linguistically and ethnically. For instance, East Pakistan (comprising a large chunk of eastern Bengal) had a substantial minority of 10 million Hindus as well as an immigrant population from West Pakistan, referred to erroneously as Biharis.[13] The latter were perceived as agents of a political and economic domination of East Pakistan by the West. Certainly, commentators agree that the relationship between the two parts of Pakistan was uneven to the point where the West treated the East as a colonial dependency, a situation exacerbated by a succession of West Pakistani, or more specifically Punjabi-led, military dictatorships. Pressure from below finally forced the military to concede free, democratic, elections in December 1970.

In Bengal, the Awami League, led by Sheikh Mujibur Rahman, campaigned around a six-point programme calling for a federal Pakistan with self-government for Bengal. It won a landslide victory which, given that it represented the largest element within Pakistan's overall population, also entitled it to form the next government. The prospect of a reorganized state was unacceptable to West Pakistan's military leaders, who immediately postponed the convening of the National Assembly. The leaders of the Awami League, despite growing popular pressure, refused to secede from Pakistan and continued to work for a negotiated settlement. Nevertheless, the military were by this time conceiving a campaign aimed at eliminating the Bengali national movement.

Nature of genocide   A build-up of troops from West Pakistan and the arrival in March 1971, in Dacca, of Tikka Khan as new governor in East Bengal were a prelude to what followed. The army attacked and then bombarded the university and city of Dacca, wiping out all potential opposition leaders, Awami League activists, professionals, students and working people. They were murdered either on the spot or in special extermination centres. Even more alarmingly, with the assistance of Jamat-i-Islami, a militant and authoritarian Islamic organization and other Bihari auxiliaries, they systematically destroyed towns and villages across large stretches of Bengal along with their inhabitants. A glaring feature of the widespread atrocities – particularly the mass rape of Bengali women – was the racial view that the Bengalis were an inferior race still infected with Hinduism. The army in time met resistance in the form of the Mukti Fauj liberation army. Some counter-massacres, notably of Biharis, followed and led in turn to further atrocities by the Pakistani army. Overall, what transpired might be described as pacificatory genocide, or genocidal massacre, though the International Commission of Jurists charged that the military's behaviour towards the Hindu minority, in terms of extermination or expulsion, amounted to a straight crime of genocide.

World response   Though events in Bengal were widely reported in the world's media, United Nations action was limited to relief efforts on behalf of the war's refugees. Both the USA and China actively supported Pakistan throughout the conflict, even providing military hardware for use in Bengal. The Soviet Union called for a halt to the bloodshed but only an Indian invasion, in December 1971, on behalf of what was now a Bengali secessionist movement, brought the conflict to an end.

Perpetrators' defence   West Pakistan's military leaders, responding to the United Nations allegations, countered that the Awami League, through an armed rebellion aided by India and designed to dismember the state of Pakistan, was to blame.

Long-term results   Bangladesh was created as a new sovereign state but only in the wake of massive dislocations and destruction caused by the war. These immense difficulties came on top of acute economic problems associated with being a very poor, densely populated third world country located in a part of the globe that is frequently exposed to natural disasters. Sheikh Mujibur Rahman led an increasingly corrupt, vengeful and dictatorial administration, until he was assassinated in 1975 by army officers in the first of a series of military coups. West Pakistan military leaders, humiliated and discredited by defeat and the loss of Bengal, slid behind a façade of democracy only to retake power again in 1977. The threat of recurring conflict with India was also exacerbated by the Bengali war, with India itself suffering acute refugee problems as a consequence of this disaster.

6   *Hutu of Burundi, 1972*

Place   Burundi, formerly part of the Belgian-administered mandate of Ruanda-Urundi, East-Central Africa.

Estimated deaths   100,000–150,000.

Immediate catalyst   Hutu rebellion against government.

Context   Process of political consolidation by minority Tutsi group over majority Hutu in the wake of decolonization.

Background   The origins of genocide in Burundi are linked to the circumstances surrounding the formation of the state following independence from the Belgian administration in 1962. As in neighbouring Rwanda, traditional society was ethnically divided along caste lines, between an 'upper' minority stratum of Tutsi pastoralists and a 'lower' majority population of Hutu agriculturalists and small traders. Relations, which were traditionally peaceful, began to break down when reforms, initiated by the Belgian trusteeship to promote elections, led to the formation and polarization of political parties on ethnic lines. In Rwanda, genocidal massacres of Tutsi by Hutu helped to ensure the latter's control. In Burundi, the situation was less clear-cut with the centralized power of the 'Mwami' (King) Mwambutsa, masking the continued Tutsi domination. In 1965, an attempted coup by Hutu officers led to a series of reprisals which virtually liquidated the Hutu political leadership, while a further coup, led by Captain Micombero, removed the Mwami. The fragility of Tutsi domination continued to be put to the test, however, particularly in April 1972, when a further Hutu rebellion erupted in the south of the country accompanied by massacres of Tutsi. The Micombero government responded with a deliberate and planned reprisal against the Hutu population.

Nature of genocide   The imposition of martial law was the smoke screen behind which the armed forces, the UPRONA Party[14] and its youth wing, the JRR,[15] conducted a 'selective genocide' against all Hutu government employees, students (including secondary school students) and business people. Catholic and Protestant Hutu priests were also killed. There was, in addition, indiscriminate slaughter which reached a peak in the month after the proclamation of martial law and continued intermittently into 1973. The clear purpose of the genocide was to consolidate Tutsi domination and remove the Hutu entirely from any positions that might challenge that ascendancy. Some 5 per cent of the population was eliminated in this way while a further 5 per cent fled to neighbouring countries.

World response   The knowledge and awareness that a genocide was taking place in Burundi was expressed in western diplomatic and governmental circles from the start. There were some weak diplomatic appeals to the Burundi government from Belgium, leading to the termination of its military cooperation, and also from the Vatican. The United Nations Commission on Human Rights reported on events and then shelved further action. France actively supported the murderous Micombero regime by providing military assistance, while the Organization of African Unity (OAU) endorsed Micombero's 'saving action' as re-establishing peace and national unity. The USA, importer of 80 per cent of Burundi's main crop, coffee, took no action.

Perpetrators' defence   The official Burundi version of events, placed before the OAU summit meeting in Rabat, in June 1972, argued that the government had acted quite legitimately against a Hutu rebellion, for which the ex-Mwami was to blame. As he had been conveniently executed at the outset of the rebellion, there was no evidence either to support or refute this charge. The implication however, was that the Hutu (the victims), not the government, were responsible for the events of 1972.

Long-term results   Burundi, one of the poorest countries in the world, remains dominated by UPRONA which has consolidated its power still further with the overthrow of Micombero in 1976. One of its policies is 'villagization', which enables it to shift peasants into new farming units in different parts of the country, ostensibly in the interests of greater production but more probably to ensure tighter control. In 1989 there was a further outbreak of genocidal violence against the Hutu majority. In 1994, acute tribal tensions between the Hutu and the Tutsi in neighbouring Rwanda spilled over into civil war and genocidal massacre (this time with the Tutsi as the principal victim) which the international community was again unable to prevent.

7   Ache Indians, 1968–72

Place   Eastern Paraguay, South America.

Estimated deaths   900.

Immediate catalyst   Government road building project through remote eastern provinces.

Context   The 'development' and exploitation by national governments and multi-national companies of South American natural resources, particularly through a policy of deforestation.

Background   The genocidal, or ethnocidal, destruction of the indige-nous peoples of the Americas is nothing very new. It has been going on since the European 'discovery' of the New World by Columbus in 1492. In this sense, the case of the Ache Indians of Paraguay is no more than a minor contemporary example of a much larger and almost relentless historical tragedy. On the other hand, it does involve elements that are decidedly 'modern'. The Ache are one of many tribes of hunters and gatherers who for centuries have existed in the tropical rain forests of South America. Students of the Ache attest to their musical and poetic attributes and to their gentleness. However, their traditionally poor, often violent, relations with the more settled Guarani people – today's majority inhabitants in Paraguay – are a reflection of their different economic lifestyle and culture. Though they share a common linguistic root, the Guarani look down on the Ache as Guayaki – rabid rats – and have traditionally enslaved or killed them in manhunts. In recent times, the state of Paraguay has been involved in bloody territorial wars with its neighbours and has been controlled by a succession of military dictatorships. The most recent, under General Alfredo Strössner, ran the country from 1954 until 1989 and had strong Nazi connections (Paraguay being one of the most notorious post-war havens for former members of the SS). Paraguay has also been heavily dependent on World Bank aid and on multi-national companies to help open up its interior in what it perceives as its development interests. The building of roads and dams thus paved the way for major lumbering projects and, when the forests were cleared, for the introduction of vast ranching *estancias*. Commercial pressure on the remaining forests, particularly as land values rose, determined that indigenous people, like the Ache, were simply in the way.

Nature of genocide Although incidents involving the death and enslavement of Ache were common prior to 1968, it was in that year that a systematic process of 'resettlement' began. Under the auspices of the Commission of Indian Affairs, a department of the Defence Ministry, the Ache were hunted down in the forest, trapped like animals and often killed by machete. Some survivors were deported to supposed reservations, notably the Colonia Nacional Guayaki, described by observers as a concentration camp. Through a combination of brutality and neglect, the denial of food and medicine, plus 'psychic shock' from their experiences, the inmates succumbed to starvation and an influenza epidemic. Adding to their misery and suffering were the activities of the 'New Tribes Mission', a North American Protestant evangelical sect which ran the reservations on the Defence Ministry's behalf. Its aim was to convert indigenous peoples to its own brand of Christianity. Amongst other things, the Ache were not allowed burial of their dead according to traditional rites of passage. Despair at the loss of their dignity and humanity led to demoralization and death. A few were 'tamed' in order to assist with the manhunts of their fellow Ache. Some women and children were sold into slavery, usually for domestic service and (or) sexual abuse.

World response The plight of the Ache was initially the concern of European and North American anthropologists, notably through the International Work Group for Indigenous Affairs, based in Copenhagen. Its lobbying in Denmark – including efforts to persuade the Danish foreign minister to intervene with the Paraguayan government – and protests by a number of concerned non-governmental organizations led to submissions in 1974 before the relevant sub-committee of the United Nations Commission on Human Rights. The charge of genocide from these groups, as well as from the Roman Catholic church in Paraguay, was unanimous. However, the committee did not pursue the matter beyond presenting submissions to the Paraguayan government. The reluctance on the part of both the United States and Soviet delegates to take any initiative was a major factor in this failure. In addition, media reports by, amongst others, the renowned traveller Norman Lewis, drawing attention in the European press to events in Eastern Paraguay, were ignored or allegedly falsified in the North American press.

Perpetrators' defence   The Paraguayan defence ministry had answers to all the charges levelled at its policy. It claimed the Ache were simply being 'relocated' for their own benefit; that the army was doing it to protect them (i.e. the Ache) from persecution; that the Ache had resisted the legal owner-occupiers of the land and that the army response was therefore only retaliatory; and, finally, that even if the Ache *were* dying, it was certainly not a case of genocide, since the United Nations Convention specified 'intent' to commit the act, which was manifestly untrue of the Paraguayan government. The American State Department backed up the Paraguayan defence, by arguing in effect that the media reports and submissions were overstated and that all was now well.

Long-term results   In 1976, anthropologists estimated that between 800 and 1,200 Ache might still be alive in the forests. In other words, around 50 per cent had been killed directly or indirectly as a result of the manhunts. The Paraguayan military turned its attention to other indigenous peoples, notably in the northern Chaco, where oil exploration was again, as in previous decades, on the agenda. Accelerated rates of deforestation and development, primarily through the auspices of governments and big companies, continue to destroy the habitat, culture and lives of native peoples, especially in South American and other tracts of surviving tropical rain forest around the globe. Though the development of Amerindian organizations and strategies for the defence of their lands and rights is rapidly on the increase, this has come too late to save the Ache and hundreds of other indigenous peoples.

8 Cambodians, 1975–79

Place   Kampuchea, formerly Cambodia, South-East Asia.

Estimated deaths   Up to 2 million.

Immediate catalyst   Take-over of power by Khmer Rouge insurgents.

Context   Escalation and spread of long-term war in South East Asia. Arrested process of decolonization.

Background   In 1969, the kingdom of Cambodia, formerly a French colony of Indo-China, became caught up in the war in neighbouring Vietnam. The United States President, Richard Nixon, in an attempt to destroy North Vietnamese supply lines to the Vietcong in South Vietnam, secretly ordered the bombing of the neutral state. This precipitated a civil war between supporters of the Americans, who took over the capital, Phnom Penh, and rebels initially led by deposed King Sihanouk. They, in turn, came to be dominated by the Khmer Rouge, a revolutionary communist and virulently anti-western group led by Pol Pot. The Khmer Rouge had a very specific programme, which included the wholesale 'deurbanization' (i.e. complete removal of the population from the cities) of Cambodia, leading to the transformation of society into a collectively organized and self-sufficent agricultural base. Commentators agree, however, that it was the brutalization of Cambodia through the massive and – until 1973 – continuous American aerial bombardment, killing or maiming hundreds of thousands and destroying the country's infrastructure, that provided the Khmer Rouge with recruits and propelled it into power. Its entry into Phnom Penh marked the end of the civil war but the opening of its campaign of terror.

Nature of genocide   Phnom Penh and all other major towns were evacuated, the urban population and refugees from the war being forced, together with peasants in the countryside, into what amounted to giant slave labour camps. Perceived enemies of the Khmer Rouge's ideology were targeted for liquidation along with their families. The victims included former officials and military personnel associated with the American-backed regime, intellectuals, business and professional people, Buddhist monks, together with minority groups such as Thais, Chinese and Vietnamese. Starvation, disease and execution is believed to have accounted for the deaths of one-quarter of Kampuchea's population under the Khmer Rouge. Opponents of the regime, including potential insurrectionists from within the ranks of the Khmer Rouge itself, were tortured and then killed in the interrogation centre, Tuol Sleng. The Khmer Rouge's cruel and cold-blooded behaviour towards its own population has sometimes been referred to as 'auto-genocide'.

World response   The American CIA had warned of a blood-bath in the event of a take-over by the Khmer Rouge. But, owing to the almost complete isolation of Kampuchea from the outside world after 1975, it took time for reports of atrocities to be authenticated. In 1979, a number of western states and the Soviet Union submitted reports to the United Nations Commission on Human Rights, effectively accusing the Khmer Rouge of perpetrating genocide. No further action, however, was taken. The Pol Pot terror was brought to an end that year by a Vietnamese invasion, which installed a new Kampuchean government under Heng Samrin.

Perpetrators' defence The Khmer Rouge consistently ignored or denied the charges of genocide brought against it. It, in turn, accused the USA of crimes against the people of Kampuchea. The Khmer's Rouge defence was, in essence, wholly ideological – namely, that the means (mass murder) had been justified by the ends (the wholesale transformation of its society).

Long-term results Cambodia remains psychologically and economically traumatized by the Pol Pot years. A massive international relief effort by voluntary agencies was successful in the wake of the Vietnamese invasion in preventing further widespread starvation. The Khmer Rouge, however, continues to remain a threat, operating guerilla attacks from refugee camps on the Thai border. Since 1979, it has formed part of a western- (and Chinese) backed alliance in opposition to the Vietnamese- and Soviet-backed regime; as such, it is actually entitled to humanitarian aid and other assistance. These international calculations mean that the Khmer Rouge also remains an influential part of the official Cambodian representation at the United Nations, while the formerly vocal western line against it has until recently been muted or entirely silent. To date, no international action has ever been taken against Pol Pot or the Khmer Rouge. Rather surprisingly, especially in light of his reported 'death' in 1996, Pol Pot emerged from the shadows in the summer of 1997, an apparent prisoner of his own Khmer Rouge, and was condemned during a show trial – though not, it must be stressed, for his unspeakable crimes of the 1970s.

9 East Timor islanders, 1975–present

Place East Timor, formerly Portuguese colony in Indonesian archipelago, South-East Asia.

Estimated deaths Between 60,000 and 200,000.

Immediate catalyst East Timor's declaration of independence followed by Indonesian invasion.

Context Indonesian state expansion in the wake of decolonization. Acute population pressures.

Background The Indonesian archipelago is a huge range of more than 13,000 islands between the Indian and Pacific oceans, its population embracing a unique cultural, ethnic and religious diversity. In the colonial era much of its territory was ruled by the Dutch East Indies Company and then directly by the Dutch state. In 1949, after a protracted struggle, Indonesia became independent under the presidency of Sukarno. He attempted to steer it towards modernity without recourse to total economic dependence on the west. However, a coup in 1965 led to the establishment of a military junta of very different, ultra-nationalist complexion. It immediately sought to consolidate its position by eliminating the Communist Party of Indonesia. This act of genocide involved the deaths of anything between 80,000 and 1 million people. Indonesia's military rulers, led by Suharto, were intent on a crash course of western-financed modernization, against the background of a rapidly expanding rural population, especially on the main island of Java. These population pressures, combined with an intense Indonesian nationalism, played a critical role in the government's expansionist intentions towards the former Dutch possession West Irian (which was absorbed in 1963) and Portuguese East Timor, which lay adjacent to Indonesian territory. In the aftermath of the overthrow of the Portuguese dictatorship in 1974, a largely undeveloped East Timor began its own process of decolonization. The two principal parties that emerged, the UDT[16] and FRETILIN[17], represented quite different approaches to independence, but Indonesian interference – ostensibly on behalf of the UDT – precipitated a civil war and the declaration of independence by the popularly backed FRETILIN group, in November 1975.

Nature of genocide Indonesian troops invaded Dili, East Timor's capital, within a few days of the declaration, strongly suggesting a deliberate and planned intention. The leaders and supporters of FRETILIN were rounded up and shot. Indiscriminate shootings and looting of Dili ensued, including the killing of ethnic Chinese, who were not party to the dispute, and supporters of UDT. FRETILIN resistance led the Indonesian army to step up its campaign against the population as a whole. Their tactics included aerial and naval bombardment, and the alleged use of poison gas, crop-burning and defoliation. Most of East Timor's population was dislocated, more than 300,000 people being 'resettled' or placed in 'transit camps', where neglect, malnutrition and the effects of disease killed at least 40,000. Torture and killings in detention centres were a further feature of the Indonesian response. Out of a population of over 600,000 in 1975, no fewer than one in ten (and in all likelihood considerably more) have since died of unnatural causes.

World response The United Nations General Assembly immediately condemned Indonesia's invasion as unlawful and reaffirmed East Timor's right to independence and self-determination. This stood in marked contrast to the actual support Indonesia received from many western nations. United States military aid proved essential to the invasion, while, in spite of the murder of some of its own nationals, Australia lent assistance by turning a blind eye to events on its northern sea borders. Reports in several Australian newspapers, however, did lead to public awareness and protests. This was reflected, too, in the single instance of a temporary arms embargo, which Sweden placed on Indonesia. Elsewhere, media coverage was generally inadequate or heavily diluted, leading to widespread ignorance of the East Timor genocide.

Perpetrators' defence Indonesia claimed its invasion was justified in order to prevent 'chaos' and 'a reign of terror' inaugurated by FRETILIN, and that it, moreover, had a 'moral obligation' to protect East Timor's people so that the 'process of decolonization could be continued'. FRETILIN's declaration of independence, it was argued, was a 'stimulus to East Indonesian secessionist movements' which would 'contribute an open invitation to meddling' by world powers. In an Australian press conference, in 1977, Indonesian Foreign Minister Adam Malik stated that between 50,000 and 80,000 East Timorese had been killed in the 'civil war' but went on to ask: 'What is the big fuss?' Most western countries, including the USA and Britain, accepted the Indonesian version of the FRETILIN 'security threat'.

Long-term results The conflict in East Timor has continued since 1975, with the continued decimation of the indigenous population, but with no end in sight to FRETILIN's resistance. There have been attempts to settle Indonesians from other islands, but these have been on a relatively small scale, given the enormity of Indonesia's population problems. The United Nations has, every year, reiterated its condemnation of Indonesia's actions but, in practice, despite opposition from Portugal and former Portuguese colonies, Indonesia's rulers can count on the USA, Australia, Britain and other western states to recognize their *de facto* control over East Timor. In spite of the extensive economic interests that western states have in the area, Indonesia remains the crippled giant of South-East Asia.

Genocide by another name?

Since the term genocide was invented, political scientists and social anthropologists have drawn attention to other ways in which human groups can be destroyed. One does not, after all, have to kill people physically to reduce them to a state of nothingness. One can simply take away their possessions and their homes, their environment, their livelihood, their culture and finally their dignity. 'Ethnocide', as it has been called, is a common world-wide phenomenon of the modern age.[18] Economic, cultural, religious, ethnic or national groups that fail to conform to the assimilatory requirements of the nation-state or its economic development can suffer its effects. In its more extreme and virulent variety, however, it can lead to 'psychic death', a stage-by-stage process of demoralization and despair which finally gives way to actual physical death (certainly during the Nazi Holocaust many Jews died – even after the war's end – primarily because their sense of human worth, and hence their will to live, had been utterly crushed). Could it be that this variety, which has been particularly applied to indigenous peoples in the path of 'modernization', is simply genocide by another name?

The destructive impulse, which has arguably always plagued human existence, has in the twentieth century reached truly awesome proportions. The inclination – and especially the ability – to express it, is in no way diminishing but, on the contrary, given technological and bureaucratic 'advances', seems to be accelerating. In an age of nuclear weapons, moreover, it may simply – and most tragically – be a stage on the road to 'omnicide', in effect the complete elimination of our species. As David Biale wrote,

> As a metaphor for a new politics of irrationality, the Holocaust contains a metaphor of inescapable relevance for a nuclear world. For the first time in human history, a government had sought to eradicate a whole people from the earth for reasons that had nothing to do with political realities. In a similar way, the idea of nuclear war lacks the most elementary political rationality, for it would necessarily destroy everything it meant to save: it would take genocide, invented in its most systematic form by the Nazis, to its global and ultimately suicidal conclusion.[19]

Notes

1 These words are attributed to Hitler in a speech delivered to his army chiefs shortly before the Nazi invasion of Poland on 1 September 1939 – alluded to in Helen Fein, *Accounting for Genocide* (The Free Press, 1979), p. 4 and cited in Margot Strom and William Parsons, *Facing History and Ourselves: Holocaust and Human Behaviour* (Intentional Educations Inc., 1982), p. 319.

2 Raphael Lemkin, *Axis Rule in Occupied Europe* (Carnegie Endowment for International Peace, 1944).

3 See Yves Ternon, 'Reflections on Genocide' in Gerard Chaliand (ed.), *Minority Peoples in the Age of Nation-States* (Pluto Press, 1989), p. 133.

4 Much of the scholarly literature on the historiography of the Holocaust focuses on the question of uniqueness versus comparability. See especially Yehuda Bauer, 'The Place of the Holocaust in Contemporary History' in Jonathan Frankel, *Studies in Contemporary Jewry*, Vol. 1 (Indiana University Press, 1984).

5 Helen Fein in I. Charney (ed.), *Towards the Understanding and Prevention of Genocide: Proceedings of the International Conference on the Holocaust and Genocide* (Westview Press, 1984).

6 Increasingly in educational and scholarly circles, the case of the Armenians is cited as the instance of genocide most closely related to the Nazi Holocaust. For

example, see Robert Melson, 'Revolutionary Genocide: On the Causes of the Armenian Genocide of 1915 and the Holocaust' in *Remembering for the Future* (Pergamon Press, 1988) and Margot Strom and William Parsons, op. cit., ch. 11.

7 For excellent analyses of the historical background to the current crisis in Northern Ireland, see R. F. Forster, *Modern Ireland, 1600–1972* (Penguin, 1988) and Paul Arthur and Keith Jeffery, *Northern Ireland Since 1968* (Basil Blackwell, 1988).

8 The complexities of the Lebanese predicament often seem impossible to unravel. One of the most penetrating and exhaustive works which renders this topic accessible is Robert Fisk, *Pity the Nation: Lebanon At War* (Andre Deutsch, 1990).

9 The progressive 'dehumanization' of the Jewish victims of Nazism between 1933 and 1941 – as a prerequisite to annihilation during the subsequent four-year period – is explored throughout Chapters 5 and 6 of Ronnie Landau, *The Nazi Holocaust* (I.B. Tauris, 1992).

10 The failure of the United Nations to invoke the Genocide Convention in the case of Cambodia and, further, the alleged participation of 'representatives' of Pol Pot's Khmer Rouge in the United Nations efforts to plan the future of Cambodia has led to widespread popular condemnation. It has consequently been suggested in certain quarters that the United Nations has somehow forfeited its right to be regarded as a serious bulwark against future genocides. See especially John Pilger's investigative newspaper and television pieces, for example *Weekend Guardian* (London), 6–7 October 1990, pp. 4–7 and *Cambodia: The Betrayal* (British ITV programme), first transmitted on 9 October 1990.

11 For specific recommended reading on the case histories, see Genocide – Select Bibliography (pp. 119–20).

12 The term 'kulak' comes from the Russian for 'fist' or 'tight fist'. In pre-Revolutionary Russia, it usually referred to a well-to-do farmer or trader. Under the Soviets, however, it came to be used as a purely derogatory description for a peasant-proprietor working for his own profit. It invariably denoted the economic exploitation of fellow-citizens and a person thus named was, virtually by definition, considered an opponent of the prevailing communist ideology.

13 Strictly speaking, Biharis come from the Indian state of Bihar, located in the north-eastern part of the country, bordering on West Bengal.

14 UPRONA is an acronym for the Parti de l'Unité et du Progres National.

15 JRR stands for Jeunesse Revolutionnaire Rwagasore. Prince Rwagasore, the eldest son of Mwami (King) Mwambutsa and UPRONA leader, had been assassinated in 1961.

16 UDT stands for Uniao Democratica Timorense.

17 FRETILIN is an acronym for Frente Revolucionaria Do Timor Leste Independente.

18 The subjects of 'ethnocide' and 'psychic death' are examined, with reference to the case of the Ache Indians, in Richard Arens (ed.), *Genocide in Paraguay* (Temple University Press, 1976).

19 David Biale, *Power and Powerlessness in Jewish History* (Schocken Books, 1988), p. 209.

Genocide – Select Bibliography

Arens, Richard (ed.), *Genocide in Paraguay* (Temple University Press, 1976)
Baxter, Craig, *Bangladesh, New Nation in an Old Setting* (Westview Press, 1984)

Chaliand, Gerard (ed.), *Minority Peoples in the Age of Nation-States* (Pluto Press, 1989)

Conquest, Robert, *Harvest of Sorrow, Soviet Collectivization and the Terror-Famine* (Hutchinson, 1986)

Conrad, Joseph, *Heart of Darkness* (Penguin, 1973)

Elliot, Gil, *Twentieth Century Book of the Dead* (Penguin, 1972)

Fein, Helen, 'Political Functions of Genocide Comparisons' in Yehuda Bauer *et al.*, *Remembering for the Future*, Vol. III (Pergamon Press, 1988)

Horowitz, Irving, *Taking Lives, Genocide and State Power* (New Brunswick, 1980)

Hughes, Robert, *The Fatal Shore* (Pan, 1987)

Katz, Steven, 'Quantity and Interpretation: Issues in the Comparative Historical Analysis of the Holocaust' in *Remembering for the Future*, Vol. III (Pergamon Press, 1988)

Kiernan, Ben, *How Pol Pot Came to Power* (Verso, 1985)

Kohen, Arnold and John Taylor, *An Act of Genocide: Indonesia's Invasion of East Timor* (Tapol, 1979)

Kuper, Leo, *Genocide, Its Political Use in the Twentieth Century* (Penguin, 1982)

Melson, Robert, 'Revolutionary Genocide: On the Causes of the Armenian Genocide of 1915 and the Holocaust' in Yehuda Bauer, *et al.*, *Remembering for the Future*, Vol. II (Pergamon Press, 1988)

Minority Rights Group, *Report No. 14, Roma: Europe's Gypsies. Report No. 15, The Amerindians of South America. Report No. 20, Burundi since the Genocide. Report No. 32, The Armenians*

Moorhead, Alan, *The Fatal Impact, the Invasion of the South Pacific, 1767–1840* (Penguin, 1968)

Ponchaud, Francois, *Cambodia Year Zero* (Penguin, 1977)

Shawcross, William, *Sideshow: Kissinger, Nixon and the Destruction of Cambodia* (Fontana, 1979)

Walker, Christopher, *Armenia, the Survival of a Nation* (Croom Helm, 1980)

PART IV

QUESTIONS, THEMES AND READING LISTS

This part contains a wide variety of questions arranged into thematic sections and sub-sections, each with its own select bibliography. (Please note that there is one comprehensive bibliography for the whole of Section 2.)

In each section there are questions intended for class discussion and debate; for personal reflection; to stimulate further research; and, at the end of each section, for formal essay response. Some questions may also form the conceptual bases of more substantial projects or individual studies (e.g. as part of A level History courses in Britain). Several questions refer expressly to documents that appear in Part II (starting on p. 49); for ease of reference, the page on which the relevant document can be found is provided in the question.

N.B. The questions that follow cover a variety of disciplines and levels, and many are open-ended. Many of these questions cannot be fully answered or, in some cases, even attempted, merely by reference to this book or, indeed, to any one book. The intention is to point the student and teacher in the right direction. Much will, of course, depend on the academic subject being studied, the background the student has in the topic and the time at the student's or class's disposal. The aim of their inclusion is to assist rather than replace the teacher! It is not to render the need for wider reading and consultation redundant.

In many instances the questions themselves have been worded in such a way as to form part of the story. Even if you feel you are not equipped to offer an informed answer, the question alone may add to your knowledge and understanding.

Historical background and context 1

The European Jew and the modern world

The following questions are intended for personal reflection, open-ended discussion, further enquiry, research and written response.

1 Why did many people, Jew and non-Jew, think that assimilation was the best means of combating or even eliminating antisemitism in Europe? Do you think that in spite of the Holocaust they are still essentially right?

2 What was the role of medieval, Church-inspired anti-Judaism in the growth of modern political and racial antisemitism?

3 What is the connection between the growth of nationalism and that of antisemitism?

4 Why do you think modern antisemitism gained a measure of respectability in certain 'enlightened' western countries during the nineteenth century?

5 In what particular respects was the expression of political antisemitism in the late-nineteenth century an omen of danger for the Jews of Europe?

6 What were the principal differences between modern antisemitism and the earlier variety of medieval anti-Judaism?

7 'Without the pogroms in Tsarist Russia during the last two decades of the nineteenth century, Zionism would have been a brief and unremarkable episode in Jewish history.' Do you agree?

8 Why do you think the *Protocols of the Elders of Zion* was so widely read and believed after the First World War? Investigate this document's history and impact in both twentieth-century Europe and the USA. (For excerpt from the Protocols, see pp. 52–55.)

9 What were the principal Jewish responses to Tsarist oppression between 1881 and the First World War?

10 Imagine it is November 1917 and you have just read the Balfour Declaration. Write a letter to *The Times* or to *The Jewish Chronicle* expressing your reaction to it. (For text of the Balfour Declaration, see pp. 55–56.)

11 To what extent were the seeds of the continuing Arab–Israeli conflict sown during the First World War?

12 To what extent was the association of Jews with the 'Red Menace' during the inter-war period a myth? How do you explain the actual level of Jewish involvement in communism and international socialism?

Modern Jewish history – select bibliography

Ben-Sasson, H. H. (ed.), *A History of the Jewish People* (Weidenfeld & Nicolson, 1976)

Bethel, Nicholas, *The Palestine Triangle* (Weidenfeld & Nicolson, 1979)

Cohn, Norman, *Warrant for Genocide: The Myth of the Jewish World-Conspiracy and the Protocols of the Elders of Zion* (Harper and Row, 1966)

Dawidowicz, Lucy, *The Golden Tradition: Jewish Life and Thought in Eastern Europe* (Holt, Rinehart and Winston, 1966)

Gilbert, Martin, *Jewish History Atlas* (Weidenfeld & Nicolson, 1976)

Katz, Jacob, *Out of the Ghetto* (Schocken Books, 1978)

Landau, Ronnie S., *The Nazi Holocaust* (I.B. Tauris, 1992), chapter 3

Laqueur, Walter, *A History of Zionism* (Weidenfeld & Nicolson, 1980)

Mendes-Flohr, Paul and Jehudah Reinharz (eds), *The Jew in the Modern World* (Oxford University Press, 1980)

Niewyk, Donald, *The Jews in Weimar Germany* (Manchester University Press, 1980)

Poliakov, Leon, *The History of Antisemitism*, 3 vols. (Vanguard Press, 1965–76)

Pulzer, Peter, *The Rise of Political Antisemitism in Germany and Austria* (John Wiley, 1964)

Sachar, Howard, *The Course of Modern Jewish History* (Delta, 1977)

Seltzer, Robert, *Jewish People, Jewish Thought. The Jewish Experience in History* (Macmillan, 1980)

Wistrich, Robert, *Antisemitism: The Longest Hatred* (Thames/Methuen, 1991)

Twentieth-century German history and the growth of Nazism

The following questions are intended for personal reflection, open-ended discussion, further enquiry, research and written response.

13 In what ways could you describe the Nazi revolution as the 'logical' or 'inevitable' outcome of German history?

14 In what ways did economic conditions in Germany following the First World War cripple the image and tenability of the Weimar Republic?

15 Some historians have described the 'war guilt clause' as one of the most damaging statements in human history. Do you agree?

16 Did the Nazi Party's overall racial philosophy have any basis in logic?

17 By what methods did the Nazi Party seek to eradicate the notion of individuality? Why was it so important to the Nazis?

18 What, in your view, were the most important components of the Nazi Party's programme and ideology?

19 Why did Nazis attach such significance to the principle of 'race and blood'?

20 How did the Nazi Party's 25-point programme show Nazi attitudes towards fundamental human rights and political freedoms? (For text of Nazi Party's 25-point programme, see pp. 57–60.)

21 Imagine you had been a German Jew living in 1920. Upon reading the 25-point programme, how would you have felt and how do you think you might have responded?

22 What, in your judgement, were the differences and points of similarity between medieval Christian attitudes and policy towards Jews and those prevailing in Nazi Germany?

23 Examine the table of Reichstag election results between 1919 and 1933 (Appendix B, p. 168). Reflect and comment on the following:

   (a) The behaviour of Catholic voters. Why do you think their parties were not so susceptible to disintegration?

   (b) The realignment and success of the left-wing parties.

   (c) The fluctuations in the Nazi vote from 1924–33.

   (d) The percentage of the German electorate voting for the Nazis throughout this period.

   (e) The two election results for 1932. In the November election the Nazis lost 34 seats and 2 million votes. How does this help explain the timing of Hitler's accession to power?

24 To what extent, if at all, can you describe the Holocaust as the product of historical phenomena and processes that were peculiarly 'German'?

25 How central was the Jewish question to the ideology of Nazism?

26 What do you think was the significance of the Jewish question in Hitler's appeal to the German electorate?

27 Why do you think the post-war German democracy was so inherently weak?

28 How vital was the Wall Street Crash and its aftermath in catapulting the Nazis to electoral prominence?

29 In which ways did the new German nationalism exclude the Jews from full acceptance in German society?

30 How did conditions in inter-war Germany produce a breeding ground for political movements of the extreme left and right?

31 To what extent can Germany's descent to totalitarianism and barbarism be attributed to a fear of Bolshevism?

Modern Germany – select bibliography

Allen, William, *The Nazi Seizure of Power: The Experience of a Single German Town* (Franklin Watts, 1984)

Arendt, Hannah, *The Origins of Totalitarianism* (Harcourt, Brace and World, 1951)

Bracher, Karl, *The German Dictatorship: The Origins, Structure and Effects of National Socialism* (Praeger, 1970)

Carr, William, *A History of Germany, 1815–1985* (Edward Arnold, 1985)

Eley, Geoff, *From Unification to Nazism* (Allen and Unwin, 1986)

Hitler, Adolf, *Mein Kampf* (Houghton Mifflin, 1943)

Jäckel, Eberhard, *Hitler's World View: A Blueprint for Power* (Harvard University Press, 1972)

Kolb, Eberhard, *The Weimar Republic* (Unwin Hyman, 1988)

Landau, Ronnie S., *The Nazi Holocaust* (I.B. Tauris, 1992), chapter 4

Massing, Paul, *Rehearsal for Destruction: A Study of Political Antisemitism in Imperial Germany* (Harper and Row, 1949)

Mosse, George, *The Crisis of German Ideology* (Grosset and Dunlop, 1964)

Noakes, Jeremy and Geoffrey Pridham, *Nazism 1919–1945. A Documentary Reader*, Vol. I (Exeter University Press, 1984)

Essay questions

1 Do you agree with the dictum: 'More than the Jews have kept the Sabbath, the Sabbath has kept the Jews'? What other ingredients in diaspora Jewish life and experience may have accounted for the durability of Jewish tradition and the sense of Jewish peoplehood?

2 'Modern antisemitism would not have developed had it not been for the emancipation of the Jews.' Assess this comment in the light of the nineteenth-century experience of the Jews.

3 'The Weimar Republic was un-German, unwelcome and ultimately unsuccessful.' To what extent do you agree with this judgement?

4 'In the past century the Jewish people have been both a major beneficiary and a major victim of European nationalism.' Comment on this verdict on the recent Jewish experience in history.

5 What is the relationship between Nazi anti-Jewish ideology and earlier expressions of anti-Judaism and antisemitism in European history?

6 To what extent was the ferocity of the Nazi onslaught rooted in the peculiar social, economic and psychological circumstances prevailing in Germany in the years following her traumatic defeat in the First World War and the humiliating Treaty of Versailles?

7 Describe the role of the Jews in modern German society, particularly during the period of the Weimar Republic. How did they react to the rising tide of Nazism during the period 1929–33?

The Holocaust: A history 2

The following questions are intended for personal reflection, open-ended class discussion, further enquiry, research and written response.

Nazi Germany (general): The early years

1 During its first year of power, by what devices did the Nazi Party strengthen its grip on Germany?
2 In your view, why did the various opposition groups prove powerless to curb Hitler?
3 Why did the Nazis turn a federal Germany into a highly centralized state?
4 What use did the Nazis make of the propaganda media in their pursuit of political and social objectives? How effective do you believe propaganda to be in the attainment of political goals?
5 Consider how the Nazis made propaganda use of the following: the Church; the radio and newspapers; schools and universities; youth groups; mass popular rallies.
6 How and why do you believe the Germans let their society be infused with Nazism?
7 Why did the Nazis allow Christianity to persist?
8 Why did the Nazis burn literature in public?

Nazi anti-Jewish legislation and policy, 1933–39

9 The Nazis' first anti-Jewish measure was the organization of an economic boycott. Why did they choose this particular action to launch their public assault?
10 Does the anti-Jewish legislation in Nazi Germany during the period 1933–38 bear any resemblance to the operation of apartheid in South Africa after 1948?
11 What objectives were achieved by the passing of the Nuremberg Laws of 1935? (For text of the Nuremberg Laws, see pp. 60–62.)
12 Why was it so vital to the success of Hitler's anti-Jewish policies that a conspicuous group be created that was disenfranchised and rightless?
13 Imagine you are one of the following:
   (a) A Jewish veteran from the First World War.
   (b) A Jew with a Christian spouse.
   (c) A Christian defined as a Jew because of Jewish grandparents.
   (d) A Christian married to a Jew.
   (e) A Christian in love with a Jew.

Describe your reactions to the publication of the Nuremberg Laws.

14 How critical do you believe the Evian conference (of 1938) to have been in determining the outcome of the Holocaust?

15 Why did the Nazis call a halt to the Kristallnacht outrages?

16 How did the rest of the world react to the Kristallnacht pogrom? (For the response of the American consul in Leipzig, see pp. 62–64.)

17 When and why did the Nazis move away from a policy of forced emigration of their Jewish population?

The context of war and Nazi anti-Jewish policy, 1939–41

18 Why do you think that only twenty years after 'the war to end all wars' the world was dragged into yet another, even more savage and destructive conflict?

19 Why did the Nazis resurrect the idea and reality of a Jewish 'ghetto'?

20 How significant was the context of war in determining a genocidal approach to the Jewish question?

21 Why did the Jews of Poland not offer resistance in the first days of Nazi occupation?

22 To what extent can Heydrich's order of 21 September 1939 be called a milestone on the road leading to the Holocaust of European Jewry? (For text of Heydrich's order of 21 September 1939, see pp. 68–69.)

23 Why did Heydrich demand that Jews be concentrated in the major cities of Poland?

24 How and why did the Nazis disguise their ultimate intentions in bureaucratic language?

25 Why were the Jewish councils established? How were they to serve Nazi goals?

26 Imagine you were a Jewish leader in Poland at the outbreak of war. How would you have interpreted the order setting up Jewish councils? Would you have cooperated? What are the reasons for your answer?

27 How did the Jewish councils become sucked into the 'Final Solution' machine?

The Holocaust: 1941–45

28 What was the Nazi leadership's purpose in holding the Wannsee Conference? (For minutes of the Wannsee Conference, see pp. 70–73.)

29 Comment on the deliberate use of euphemistic language at the Wannsee Conference.

30 Why were no objections raised at the Wannsee Conference?

31 What is the historical significance of the Wannsee Conference and our records of it?

32 Why was there no clear, unequivocal order that every Jew in Europe was to be killed?

33 Why did the Nazis proceed with greater circumspection in their assault upon the Jews of western European countries than they did in eastern Europe?

34 Could a 'Final Solution' – even one limited to Germany, Austria and Czechoslovakia – conceivably, in your view, have been implemented before September 1939? Before 1941?

35 What reasons did the Nazis have for choosing Poland as the location for their extermination camps?

36 Why did a higher proportion of Jews survive in Fascist Italy and in countries allied to Germany, such as Rumania and Hungary, than in, for example, anti-Nazi Holland with its democratic tradition and long history of toleration towards Jews?

37 Why did so many Jews die in Poland? Does the explanation lie in the religious antisemitism of the indigenous population? Or is the answer much more complex?

The Holocaust: A history – select bibliography

Arad, Yitzhak, Yisrael Gutman and Abraham Margaliot (eds), *Documents on The Holocaust: Selected Sources of the Destruction of the Jews of Germany, Poland and the Soviet Union* (Yad Vashem Publications, 1981)

Arendt, Hannah, *The Origins of Totalitarianism* (Harcourt, Brace and World, 1951)

Bauer, Yehuda, *The History of the Holocaust* (Franklin Watts, 1982)

Broszat, Martin, *The Hitler State* (Longman, 1981)

Browning, Christopher, *The Path to Genocide* (Cambridge University Press, 1992)

Bullock, Alan, *Hitler: A Study in Tyranny* (Penguin, 1962)

Burleigh, Michael, *Death and Deliverance: 'Euthanasia' in Germany, 1900–1945* (Cambridge University Press, 1994)

Cesarani, David (ed.), *The Final Solution: Origins and Implementation* (Routledge, 1994)

Dawidowicz, Lucy, *The War Against the Jews* (Penguin, 1975)

Donat, Alexander, *The Holocaust Kingdom* (Holt, Rinehart and Winston, 1965)

Evans, Richard, *In Hitler's Shadow: West German Historians and the Attempt to Escape from the Nazi Past* (I. B. Tauris, 1991)

Facing History and Ourselves: Resource Book – Holocaust and Human Behaviour (Facing History and Ourselves National Foundation, 1994)

Friedlander, Albert (ed.), *Out of the Whirlwind: A Reader of Holocaust Literature* (Schocken Books, 1976)

Friedlander, Henry, *The Origins of Nazi Genocide: From Euthanasia to The Final Solution* (University of North Carolina Press, 1995)

Gilbert, Martin, *Atlas of the Holocaust* (Routledge, 1993)

Gilbert, Martin, *The Holocaust: The Jewish Tragedy* (Collins, 1986)

Hilberg, Raul, *The Destruction of the European Jews* (Quadrangle Books, 1961)

Katz, Steven T. *The Holocaust in Historical Perspective* (Oxford University Press, 1993)

Kershaw, Ian, *The Nazi Dictatorship: Problems and Perspectives of Interpretation* (Routledge, 1993)

Landau, Ronnie S., *The Nazi Holocaust* (I.B. Tauris, 1992), chapters 5–7

Marrus, Michael, *The Unwanted: European Refugees in the Twentieth Century* (Oxford University Press, 1985)

Marrus, Michael, *The Holocaust in History* (Penguin, 1987)

Noakes, Jeremy and Geoffrey Pridham (eds), *Nazism 1919–1945. A Documentary Reader*, 4 vols. (Exeter University Press, Vols. I & II 1984, Vol. III 1988 and Vol. IV 1997)

Robinson, Jacob, *And the Crooked Shall Be Made Straight* (Macmillan, 1968)

Supple, Carrie, *From Prejudice to Genocide: Teaching the Holocaust* (Trentham Books, 1993)

Essay questions

1 How, why and when did the Nazis determine a policy of total annihilation of the Jews of Europe?

2 What were the successive phases in Nazi policy towards the Jews, culminating in mass murder? What were the major turning-points in the evolution of Nazi Jewish policy?

3 What were the similarities and the differences between the Jewish experience of Nazism and that of the five and a half million other civilians – Gypsies, Poles, Russians, homosexuals, Jehovah's Witnesses and others – who were also murdered in cold blood?

4 Could the Holocaust have happened without the person and personality of Adolf Hitler?

5 What do you understand by the term 'war crime'? Was the extermination of European Jewry between 1941 and 1945 a 'war crime'?

3 Themes, issues and protagonists

The perpetrators

The following questions are intended for personal reflection, open-ended class discussion, further enquiry, research and written response.

1. What do you understand by the term 'cold cult of professionalism'? Does this, in your view, offer any explanation for an individual's involvement in mass murder?

2. In Himmler's address to his SS officers, why did he commend their discretion and silence over the Jewish policy? Was he not 'proud' of their actions? (For text of Himmler's speech, see pp. 78–79.)

3. If the mass annihilation of Jews was so desirable and 'glorious', why were so many written records and other physical evidence of the Holocaust destroyed by the Nazis?
4. What picture does Dr Kremer's diary convey about the world of Auschwitz? (For text of diary, see pp. 77–78)
5. What, in your view, is the significance as an historical document of Dr Kremer's diary?
6. How was it possible for certain individuals, whose role would prove indispensable to the carrying out of the 'Final Solution of the Jewish question', to be subtly conditioned into believing that to kill Jews was morally no worse than to brush dandruff off their jackets – and, on the contrary, was a morally acceptable thing?

The perpetrators – select bibliography

Arendt, Hannah, *Eichmann in Jerusalem: A Report on the Banality of Evil* (Penguin, 1983)
Bullock, Alan, *Hitler: A Study in Tyranny* (Penguin, 1962)
Facing History and Ourselves: Resource Book – Holocaust and Human Behaviour (Facing History and Ourselves National Foundation, 1994)
Fein, Helen, *Accounting for Genocide: National Responses and Jewish Victimization during the Holocaust* (The Free Press, 1979)
Hitler, Adolf, *Mein Kampf* [Translated by R. Manheim], (Houghton Mifflin, 1943)
Landau, Ronnie S., *The Nazi Holocaust* (I.B. Tauris, 1992), chapter 8
Lifton, Robert and Eric Markhusen, *The Genocidal Mentality: The Nazi Holocaust and the Nuclear Threat* (Macmillan, 1991)
Marrus, Michael, *The Holocaust in History* (Penguin, 1987)
Milgram, Stanley, *Obedience to Authority* (Harper and Row, 1974)
Noakes, Jeremy and Geoffrey Pridham (eds), *Nazism 1919–1945. A Documentary Reader*, 4 vols., (Exeter University Press, Vols. I & II 1984, Vol. III 1988 and Vol. IV 1997)
Sereny, Gitta, *Into That Darkness: From Mercy Killing to Mass Murder* (Andre Deutsch, 1974)
Sereny, Gitta, *Albert Speer: His Battle with Truth* (Macmillan, 1995)
Speer, Albert, *Inside the Third Reich: Memoirs* (Macmillan, 1970)
Supple, Carrie, *From Prejudice to Genocide: Teaching the Holocaust* (Trentham Books, 1993)

The victims

The following questions are intended for personal reflection, open-ended discussion, further enquiry, research and written response.

7 Once the Jewish council leadership knew for certain the meaning of 'deportation', why did some still persist in their cooperation?
8 At what point would you say, of the Jewish Council leadership, that 'cooperation' became 'collaboration'?

9 Why did the majority of Jews appear to allow themselves to be transported to their deaths at Treblinka, Auschwitz and other annihilation camps?

10 'Armed resistance in Eastern Europe was suicidal.' Do you agree?

11 What factors militated against a truly successful Jewish armed resistance?

12 How might resistance have been different in a ghetto, in a camp or as a partisan?

13 What forms of resistance were there other than that involving the use of arms?

14 What arguments might have been used by those opposed to armed resistance to the Nazis in a) the ghettos?; b) the camps?

The victims – select bibliography

Arad, Yitzhak, Yisrael Gutman and Abraham Margaliot (eds), *Documents on The Holocaust* (Yad Vashem Publications, 1981)

Dobroszycki, Lucjan, *The Chronicle of the Lodz Ghetto, 1941–44*, (Yale University Press, 1984)

Donat, Alexander, *The Holocaust Kingdom* (Holt, Rinehart and Winston, 1965)

Friedlander, Albert (ed.), *Out of the Whirlwind: A Reader of Holocaust Literature* (Schocken Books, 1976)

Gilbert, Martin, *Atlas of the Holocaust* (Routledge, 1993)

Gilbert, Martin, *The Holocaust: The Jewish Tragedy* (Collins, 1986)

Gross, Leonard, *The Last Jews of Berlin* (Bantam Books, 1983)

Kaplan, Chaim, *The Warsaw Ghetto Diary of Chaim A. Kaplan* (Collier Books, 1973)

Landau, Ronnie S., *The Nazi Holocaust*, (I.B. Tauris, 1992), chapter 8

Levi, Primo, *If This Is A Man/The Truce* (Penguin, 1979)

Marrus, Michael, *The Holocaust in History* (Penguin, 1987)

Pisar, Samuel, *Of Blood and Hope* (Cassel, 1980)

Sternberg, Lucien, *Not As a Lamb* (Saxon House, 1970)

Supple, Carrie, *From Prejudice to Genocide: Teaching the Holocaust* (Trentham Books, 1993)

Trunk, Isaiah, *Jewish Responses to Nazi Persecution* (Stein and Day, 1979)

Trunk, Isaiah, *Judenrat: The Jewish Councils in Eastern Europe Under Nazi Occupation* (Macmillan, 1972)

The bystanders

The following questions are intended for personal reflection, open-ended discussion, further enquiry, research and written response.

15 Why did the British government introduce the White Paper of 1939, which strictly curtailed Jewish immigration to Palestine? In the light of what we now know of later events, was this, in your view, a significant action?

16 Why was the protest of church leaders against the persecution and

eventual extermination of the Jews not more vociferous and more effective?

17 Why did the Pope maintain his silence? Is it reasonable to have expected the Pope to have come to the rescue of Jews? Do you feel he could have done more? Would the executioners' hand in any case have been stayed by his intervention?

18 Why didn't the International Red Cross do more to alleviate the plight of European Jewry?

19 What arguments could be made for and against the claim that the Allies ought to have bombed Auschwitz?

20 In your view, were the people of Nazi-occupied Europe less, or more, responsible for the catastrophe that overwhelmed the Jews than the people of the free world?

21 Why do you think the anti-Nazi Polish underground failed to provide proper assistance to the suffering Jewish population – even during the Warsaw Ghetto uprising of 1943?

22 How big a factor is the astonishing human capacity for indifference to the plight of others (present in all societies and arguably on the increase) in explaining the path to Auschwitz and Treblinka?

The bystanders – select bibliography

Bankier, David, *The Germans and the Final Solution* (Basil Blackwell, 1992)

Davies, A. J., *Antisemitism and the Christian Mind* (New York, 1969)

Fein, Helen, *Accounting for Genocide: National Responses and Jewish Victimization during the Holocaust* (The Free Press, 1979)

Gilbert, Martin, *Auschwitz and the Allies* (Michael Joseph, 1982)

Kershaw, Ian, *Popular Opinion and Political Dissent in the Third Reich* (Oxford University Press, 1983)

Kushner, Tony, *The Holocaust and the Liberal Imagination* (Basil Blackwell, 1994)

Landau, Ronnie S., *The Nazi Holocaust* (I.B. Tauris, 1992), chapter 8

Laqueur, Walter, *The Terrible Secret. Suppression of the Truth about Hitler's 'Final Solution'* (Penguin, 1980)

Marrus, Michael, *The Unwanted: European Refugees in the Twentieth Century* (Oxford University Press, 1985)

Marrus, Michael, *The Holocaust in History* (Penguin, 1987)

Supple, Carrie, *From Prejudice to Genocide: Teaching the Holocaust* (Trentham Books, 1993)

Wasserstein, Bernard, *Britain and the Jews of Europe, 1939–1945* (Institute of Jewish Affairs, 1979)

Wyman, David, *The Abandonment of the Jews: America and the Holocaust, 1941–45* (Pantheon Books, 1984)

Aftermath, impact and lessons of the Holocaust

The following questions are intended for personal reflection, open-ended discussion, further enquiry, research and written response.

23 Why did so many Jewish survivors experience so little joy in liberation?

24 Why did so many Holocaust survivors opt to go to Palestine after the war?

25 In your opinion, would there have been a State of Israel had it not been for the Holocaust?

26 Many writers have claimed that the Holocaust has imposed special obligations on the surviving Jews of the world, especially in respect of:

(a) future Jewish survival;

(b) support for the State of Israel;

(c) treatment of the Palestinian people and *their* rights to a land.

Do you agree that these are 'special obligations'? Whether you agree or not, in what ways do you believe such 'obligations' might be in conflict with each other?

27 What are the principal changes in the demographic map of world Jewry as a result of the Holocaust?

28 Some sceptics, 'revisionists' and neo-Nazis, for their different reasons, today deny that the Holocaust involved mass murder on such a wide scale. In some extreme instances, they claim that it never took place at all, but was a Jewish (or Zionist) 'hoax'. Their assertions are frequently based on the absence of a written order signed by Hitler. How would you respond to such claims?

29 It has been said that the most important lessons of the Holocaust are: do not be a perpetrator; do not be a victim; and do not be a bystander.

Do you agree that these are the most crucial general messages conveyed by this historical event? Have there been any times in your own life when you may have fallen – even to a very limited extent – into one of these categories? Consider and discuss the circumstances and possible motives behind such 'perpetration', 'victimization' or 'bystanding'.

30 Are there any other historical instances of 'genocide' that bear points of resemblance with the Holocaust?

31 In the light of your reading of Part III 'Genocide in the Modern Era' (pp. 89–120), what features, if any, do a) the perpetrators of different genocides and b) the victims of different genocides appear to have in common with each other?

Aftermath, impact and lessons of Holocaust
– select bibliography

Bauer, Yehuda, *The Holocaust in Historical Perspective* (Sheldon Press, 1978)

Bauman, Zygmunt, *Modernity and the Holocaust* (Polity Press, 1989)

Biale, David, *Power and Powerlessness in Jewish History* (Schocken Books, 1988)

Bower, Tom, *Blind Eye To Murder: Britain, America and the Purging of Nazi Germany – A Pledge Betrayed* (Andre Deutsch, 1981)

Chaliand, Gerard (ed.), *Minority Peoples in the Age of Nation-States* (Pluto Press, 1989)

Elliot, Gil, *Twentieth Century Book of the Dead* (Penguin, 1972)

Evans, Richard, *In Hitler's Shadow: West German Historians and the Attempt to Escape from the Nazi Past* (I. B. Tauris, 1991)

Fackenheim, Emil, *The Jewish Return into History* (Schocken Books, 1978)

Hughes, Robert, *The Fatal Shore* (Pan, 1987)

Insdorf, Annette, *Indelible Shadows: Film and the Holocaust* (Cambridge University Press, 1989)

Landau, Ronnie S., *The Nazi Holocaust* (I.B. Tauris, 1992), chapter 10

Lifton, Robert and Eric Markhusen, *The Genocidal Mentality: The Nazi Holocaust and the Nuclear Threat* (Macmillan, 1991)

Lipstadt, Deborah, *Denying the Holocaust: The Growing Assault on Truth and Memory* (The Free Press, 1993)

Marrus, Michael, *The Holocaust in History* (Penguin, 1987)

Rubenstein, Richard, *The Cunning of History* (Harper Colophon, 1975)

Young, James, *The Texture of Memory: Holocaust Memorials and Meaning* (Yale University Press, 1993)

Essay questions

1 Comment on the motives and behaviour of the perpetrators in the light of your understanding of the terms 'morality', 'normality' and 'civilization'.

2 'The road to Auschwitz was built on hate but paved with indifference' (Ian Kershaw). How significant was the role of 'indifference' – on the part of various groups and individuals – in determining the final, terrible outcome?

3 'The role of the leaders in the destruction of their own people is undoubtedly the darkest chapter of the whole dark story' (Hannah Arendt). How far do you agree with this verdict?

4 Describe and account for the incidence of Jewish armed resistance during the Second World War.

5 'The Holocaust is the ultimate example thus far of twentieth-century man's misuse of technology and bureaucracy.' Comment on this verdict.

6 Assess the postwar impact – physically, politically and psychologically – of the Holocaust on the Jews of the world.

7 Look carefully at the 'Prejudice' chart in Appendix F (p. 175). In what ways does the tragic story of the Holocaust – including its historical,

social and psychological aspects – fit into the larger picture of human bigotry, hatred and prejudice? How would you relate the causes, thinking and possible motives behind the Holocaust to the problems of racism in today's society?

8 Is the catastrophe that overwhelmed the Jews of Europe an incomparably unique historical phenomenon or is it a case within the category of 'genocide'?

PART V

HISTORY OF THE HOLOCAUST

A chronological outline (1933–45)

1933

30 January	Hitler appointed Chancellor. In the following weeks and months the Nazis assume total control of German state, abolishing its federalist structure, dismantling democratic government and outlawing political parties and trades unions.
20 March	Dachau concentration camp set up on Himmler's orders. First inmates include communists, socialists, homosexuals and Jews.
1 April	Nazi boycott of Jewish businesses and professions accompanied by a wave of terror.
7 April	'Restoration of the Professional Civil Service Act' dismisses Jews and those considered politically undesirable from the civil service.
22 April	Jews disqualified from working in hospitals.
25 April	'Law against the Overcrowding of German Schools' begins the elimination of Jewish teachers and pupils from German schools system.
10 May	Public book-burning in Berlin organized by Goebbels targets 'Jewish' books and other books considered 'degenerate' by the Nazis.
August	'Ha'avara' (transfer) agreement between German Ministry of Economics and Zionist Organization facilitates large-scale emigration of Jews from Germany to Palestine.
29 September	Hereditary farm law bans Jews from ownership of land. On the same day a further law bans Jews from all aspects of German cultural and sporting life.

1934

1 May	Nazi propaganda weekly *Der Stürmer* revives ritual murder accusation against Jews.
30 June	Murder of Röhm and other SA leaders in the 'Night of the Long Knives'.
2 August	Death of President Hindenburg. Hitler declares himself Führer.

1935

15 September	Hitler uses the occasion of the Nazi rally in Nuremberg to issue the Nuremberg Laws: (i) 'Reich Citizenship Law' which removes Jewish equality before the law; and (ii) 'Law for the Protection of German Blood and Honour' which prohibits marriage or sexual relations between Jews and non-Jews.

1 November	Supplement to the 'Reich Citizenship Law' disqualifies Jews from German citizenship. Thirteen days later a further supplement defines categories of 'Mischling' or 'part Jews'.

1936

March	Spate of anti-Jewish pogroms in Poland, abetted by an inflammatory speech by Polish Cardinal Hlond against Jewish 'usury, fraud and white slavery'.
August	Anti-Jewish discriminatory measures eased during Olympic Games in Berlin, but re-applied and extended after their conclusion to cover all areas of economic and social activity.

1937

19 July	Buchenwald concentration camp established.

1938

12 March	Nazi troops enter Vienna, effecting Austrian *Anschluss* with Germany. Rash of antisemitic incidents follow. German anti-Jewish laws swiftly applied to new province. Austrian Jews flee in their thousands.
28 March	Personal property of German Jews over 5,000 marks in value to be officially registered – first of a series of regulations aimed at registering all Jewish-owned domestic and foreign property, as a prelude to confiscation by the state.
4 May	Hungarian government introduces *numerus clausus* restricting Jewish entry into liberal professions, administration, commerce and industry.
14 June	All Jewish firms in Germany to be registered with the Ministry of Economics.
6–15 July	International conference held at Evian in France discusses and fails to find solution to Jewish refugee problem precipitated by the *Anschluss*.
25 July	Licences of Jewish doctors cancelled.
August	Eichmann opens a Vienna office for Jewish emigration.
17 August	Jewish women have to add 'Sarah' and Jewish men 'Israel' to their first names for official purposes.
September–October	Munich crisis culminates in Anglo-French decision to cede Czech Sudetenland to the Germans. Nazi occupation the following month leads to mass flight of Jews from region.

27 September	Licences of Jewish lawyers cancelled.
5 October	Following confiscation of Jewish passports, new passports to Jews now issued with suffix 'J'. This followed a Swiss suggestion to make it easier for the Swiss border police to recognize which refugees seeking asylum were political refugees to be admitted, or Jews to be denied permission to entry.
28 October	17,000 Polish-born Jews living in Germany expelled.
7 November	Herschl Grynszpan assassinates German official in Paris in response to the expulsion of his parents.
9–10 November	Kristallnacht, the Nazi response to the assassination. Night-long campaign of violence and physical destruction against synagogues and shops leaves 91 dead. Jews held responsible by Nazis; *c.* 25,000 sent to concentration camps. 1,000 million marks required of Jews in 'reparations'.
12 November	Göring convenes conference of Nazi officials to plan the complete 'Aryanization' of Jewish businesses in Germany.
16 November	Decree forbids Jewish children to attend German schools. From now on they may only attend Jewish schools.

1939

24 January	Heydrich assigned by Göring to remove all Jews from Reich through emigration. The *Reichsvertretung*, the Jewish representative organization in Nazi Germany, reformed as the *Reichsvereinigung* (State Association) under Nazi supervision for this purpose.
30 January	Hitler delivers Reichstag speech in which he threatens that if international Jewry plunge the world into war (*sic*), the Jews of Europe will be annihilated.
21 February	Decree requires Jews to surrender all gold and silver in their possession.
15 March	German troops enter Prague, absorbing formerly Czech provinces of Bohemia and Moravia into Greater Germany. Leads to mass flight of Czech Jews. Eichmann sets up a Jewish emigration office in Prague. Slovakia becomes independent ally of Nazi Germany.
21 March	German troops occupy Lithuanian-administered Memel. Jewish population flees.
30 April	Revocation of tenancy protection for Jews paves way for their relocation in 'communal Jewish houses'.
May	British government White Paper sets a limit for entry of

	75,000 Jewish refugees into Palestine over following five years.
22 August	Hitler's speech to generals urges liquidation of Poles in forthcoming war in order to gain *Lebensraum* for Germany.
23 August	Non-aggression Pact between Nazi Germany and the Soviet Union, which includes secret conditions for the division of Eastern Europe, prepares the way for the Nazi attack on Poland.
1 September	Nazi invasion of Poland accompanied by accelerating violence against both Poles and Jews. *Einsatzgruppen* begin executions of Poles. German Jews placed under curfew and have radio sets confiscated.
3 September	Britain and France declare war on Germany.
21 September	Beginning of dissolution of traditional Polish Jewish communities. Parallel movement towards enforced resettlement of Jews in ghettos. Order for expulsion of all Jews and Gypsies from areas of Poland annexed to Greater Germany.
28 September	Total defeat of Poland leads to partition between Nazi Germany and the Soviet Union under terms of Non-aggression Pact.
October	Euthanasia programme begins, leading to the deaths of over 70,000 mentally and physically disabled people by August 1941.
23 November	All Jews in Nazi-occupied Europe required to wear yellow Star of David.
28 November	Jewish Councils (*Judenräte*) ordered into existence in German-occupied Poland.
12 December	Labour camps set up throughout German-occupied Poland. All Jewish males between 14 and 60 required for forced labour.

1940

9 April	German blitzkrieg in the west begins.
1 May	The Lodz Ghetto, containing 160,000 Jews and with Chaim Rumkowski at its head, is sealed off from outside world.
22 June	France defeated. Petain sues for peace leading to creation of collaborative Vichy government in the south.
July	German Foreign Office proposes that European Jews be deported to French Madagascar.
October	Deportations into Warsaw Ghetto begin. Wall is built to

isolate Jews from rest of city. By early 1941, 400,000 are confined here in rapidly deteriorating conditions.

3 October Vichy government debars Jews from public offices and most areas of French economic life, and a day later authorizes internment of foreign Jews. Similar anti-Jewish legislation enacted by Antonescu regime in Rumania.

1941

January Major anti-Jewish pogrom by Rumanian fascist Iron Guard in Bucharest.

February Deportations of several hundred Dutch Jews to Buchenwald and Sachsenhausen concentration camps in reprisal for the self-defence killing of a Dutch Nazi. Two-day general strike in Amsterdam in support of Jews is crushed.

1 March Himmler sets in motion plans for expansion of Auschwitz complex.

6 April German invasion of Yugoslavia and Greece triggers pogroms against Jews and Serbs, carried out by pro-Nazi militia in Croatia.

May Beginning of internment of foreign-born Jews in Paris.

4 June German army directive to troops about to invade the Soviet Union to eliminate all resistance. Jews are included in this category. Commissar Order two days later spells out that all Soviet officials are to be liquidated.

22 June Operation Barbarossa, the invasion of the Soviet Union by Nazi Germany and her Hungarian, Rumanian and Finnish allies. Precipitates local massacres of Jews in Baltic States and the western Ukraine. Four commandos of *Einsatzgruppen* begin mass slaughter of Jews, Gypsies and Soviet officials.

22 July Vichy government commences expropriation of French Jewish businesses.

31 July Heydrich receives orders from Göring, on Hitler's instructions, to begin preparations for the 'intended Final Solution of the Jewish Question'.

August Rumanians begin expelling Jews from Bessarabia and Bukovina, which they had re-occupied on Operation Barbarossa, into Transnistria across the river Dneister. Thousands perish on death marches.

23 August Hitler officially calls off euthanasia programme after Bishop von Galen's denunciatory sermon on the subject.

26 August	Bloody massacre of Hungarian Jewish refugees by SS units and Ukrainian militia at Kamenets Podolsk in the Ukraine. Mass executions throughout Nazi-occupied Soviet regions intensify.
September	Zyclon B Gas tested for the first time at Auschwitz on Soviet prisoners of war. Construction of killing centre at Birkenau (adjacent to existing Auschwitz complex) begins.
6 September	Vilna Jews ghettoized.
29–30 September	Bloodbath in Babi Yar gorge, near the Ukrainian capital of Kiev. Jews and Gypsies butchered by SS units and Ukrainian militia.
14 October	Mass deportations of Jews from Greater Germany to the east begins. Thousands are shot on arrival.
23 October	Nazi emigration policy towards Jews officially ends. No more Jews allowed to leave the Reich or Nazi sphere of influence. Concurrently Rumanian troops perpetrate horrendous massacre of Jews in Black Sea port of Odessa.
24 November	New 'model' ghetto created at Theresienstadt for thousands of Central European Jews.
30 November	Executions of Riga Jews in the Rumbuli forest.
December	Generalplan Ost (general plan for the East), drawn up under Himmler's directions, proposes deportation of 31 million non-Germans in conquered east to make *Lebensraum* for German colonists.
5 December	Soviet counter-offensive in front of Moscow signals failure of Operation Barbarossa.
8 December	Gas killings of Jews and Gypsies in mobile vans begin in Chelmno, western Poland.
11 December	Following Japanese bombing of Pearl Harbour, Germany declares war on the USA.

1942

January	Jewish resistance and partisan groups organized in Vilna and Kovno.
20 January	The Wannsee Conference in Berlin. Nazi officials agree plans for the coordination of the 'Final Solution'.
24 February	The ship *Struma*, carrying Jewish refugees from Rumania, having been refused permission to sail to British-controlled Palestine is sunk in the Black Sea. All bar one passenger are drowned.
16 March	Operation Reinhard, the liquidation of Polish Jewry, begins. First transports to Belzec, Sobibor, Majdanek and Treblinka death camps.

24 March	First deportations of Jews to Auschwitz, from Slovakia. Followed four days later by first Jewish refugees from France.
2 June	BBC broadcasts extracts from a report smuggled out of Poland by the Jewish socialist Bund. It tells of extermination of 700,000 Jews at Chelmno and elsewhere.
9 June	Mobile gas van killings begin in Riga, Latvia.
10 June	Czech village of Lidice liquidated in revenge for the assassination of SS chief Heydrich. Additional round-ups of Czechs in Prague and Jews in Berlin.
14 July	Mass deportation of Dutch Jews to Auschwitz begins, followed shortly afterwards by Jews from Belgium and Luxembourg.
22 July	Deportation of Warsaw Jews to Treblinka death camp begins.
28 July	Underground Jewish Combat Organization formed in Warsaw Ghetto.
8 August	Gerhardt Riegner, the World Jewish Congress representative in Geneva, sends telegram to British and American governments with information about the 'Final Solution'.
15 October	Horrendous slaughter of Jews by SS in Brest-Litovsk, Soviet Russia.
25 October	Deportation of Norwegian Jews to Auschwitz begins, despite resistance and escape routes provided by many Norwegians.
2 November	Start of major round-up of all Jews in Bialystok region of Poland. 170,000 killed in one week.
4 November	Tide of war turns with British victory at El Alamein, followed on 19 November by Russian counter-offensive at Stalingrad.
27 November	Mass expulsion of Poles from Zamosc region of Poland to provide '*lebensraum*' for Germans.
16 November	Deportations of German Gypsies to Auschwitz begins.
17 November	Inter-Allied declaration denounces murder of European Jewry and states that those responsible will be punished.
1943	
January	Jewish transport to Treblinka attacks guards on arrival.
8 March	Deportations of Greek Jews to Treblinka (and later Auschwitz) begins.
14 March	Cracow Ghetto liquidated.
17 March	Bulgarian Parliament vetoes proposed deportation of Bulgarian Jews to the death camps.

5 April	Massacres of Lithuanian Jews in Pónary woods.
19 April	Warsaw Ghetto uprising begins as SS finalizes plans for its complete liquidation. At the same time, Bermuda Conference of American and British officials fails to implement plans for rescue of European Jewry or to provide assistance for European refugees.
12 May	In despair at his failure to gain Allied military assistance for the uprising, Bundist leader Shmuel Zygielboym commits suicide in London. Liquidation of the Warsaw Ghetto is completed.
June	Himmler's Unit 1005 slave labour battalions begin work exhuming corpses from death camps and execution sites in order to obliterate evidence of the Holocaust.
21 June	Lwow Ghetto liquidated.
1 July	Final order of Reich Citizenship Act removes all legal protection from the Jews of Germany.
2 August	Attempted mass revolt and break-out from Treblinka crushed.
16 August	Bialystok Ghetto liquidated. Attempted Jewish revolt is put down.
September–October	Danes sabotage Nazi deportation plans for Danish Jews, most of whom are ferried to safety in neutral Sweden.
23 September	Vilna Ghetto liquidated.
14 October	Partial break-out of Jews and Soviet prisoners of war from Sobibor.
16 October	Deportation of Italian Jews to Auschwitz begins following Nazi occupation of northern Italy.
1944	
22 January	United States President Roosevelt sets up War Refugees Board to assist relief and rescue efforts.
19 March	Nazis occupy Hungary following fears that the Hungarian regime is about to sue for peace with the Allies. Eichmann arrives to supervise anti-Jewish measures.
May	Proposals from Jewish leaders to Allies that they bomb railway lines leading to Auschwitz.
15 May	Deportations of Hungarian Jews to Auschwitz begins and quickly accelerates as Red Army breaks into eastern Hungary.
6 June	Allies open 'Second Front' with Normandy landings.
8 June	International pressure from Sweden, the Red Cross, the Vatican and the Allies leads to Hungarian government

halting deportations. Eichmann concurrently involved in negotiations with Jewish leaders, offering to exchange lives of Hungarian Jews for war materials.

20 July	Bomb plot to assassinate Hitler fails.
23 July	Red Army advance liberates Majdanek concentration camp in Poland coinciding with large-scale German evacuations of death camp inmates to Dachau, Bergen-Belsen and Stutthof.
6 August	70,000 remaining Jews in Lodz, including the Judenrat leader Chaim Rumkowski, are deported to Auschwitz (except for several hundred Jews who are mysteriously left behind).
7 October	Inmates blow up one of the four Auschwitz crematoria in abortive and suicidal revolt – conducted by Jewish inmates against express direction of general prisoner underground.
15 October	The Arrow Cross, the Hungarian fascist party, stages successful coup in Budapest in the Nazi interest.
2 November	Swedish diplomat Raoul Wallenberg intervenes to save 4,000 Budapest Jews as SS and Arrow Cross begin six-day orgy of mass murder.
28 November	Last gassings in Auschwitz. Himmler orders gas chambers to be destroyed.

1945

January	Death marches of Jewish and non-Jewish slave labour from east towards Germany at their height.
28 January	Auschwitz-Birkenau complex liberated by Red Army.
March–April	Himmler in series of secret negotiations with Swedish Red Cross and with Jewish World Congress to stop the continuing concentration camp killings.
11 April	Buchenwald liberated by American troops.
15 April	British troops liberate Bergen-Belsen. Reality of Nazi atrocities send shock waves throughout the world. Simultaneously, SS death march evacuations continue from camps still under Nazi control.
25 April	Soviet and American forces meet on the Elbe. Red Army engages German army remnants in Berlin.
28 April	Dachau liberated.
30 April	Hitler commits suicide in his Berlin bunker, after dictating a last political testament in which he blames international Jewry for Germany's downfall.
2 May	Berlin captured by Red Army.
1–5 May	Continuing death marches in diminishing Nazi enclave.

8 May   Nazi Germany surrenders unconditionally to Allies. War in Europe ends but many liberated camp survivors continue to die from malnutrition, sickness and exhaustion.

PART VI

REFERENCE SECTIONS

Basic terms for understanding the Holocaust

Anschluss Literally 'union' or 'joining together'. In this case, Austria's annexation by Hitler's Germany on 12 March 1938.

Blitzkrieg German term, literally meaning 'lightning war', used to describe the intensity and speed of German military onslaught upon enemies' territory.

Bund Jewish socialist movement founded in Tsarist Russia in 1897. Committed to secular non-territorial nationalism, Jewish cultural and linguistic (Yiddish) autonomy, and strongly antagonistic to Zionism (for which, see below).

Concentration camp A camp for detention of perceived enemies of the Nazi state. Originally set up after Hitler's accession to power in 1933, the concentration camp regime involved forced labour and systematic use of terror. Massively extended to territories and people coming under Nazi occupation during the war, usually with a high percentage of Jewish prisoners.

Death camp As distinct from both labour and concentration camps, a centre whose sole purpose was to annihilate its inmates. The main Nazi death camps were sited on Polish soil – Auschwitz-Birkenau, Belzec, Chelmno, Majdanek, Sobibor and Treblinka.

Death marches The evacuation and forced marches of camp inmates during the latter stages of the war, when the Nazis felt themselves threatened by the proximity of Allied troops. Tens of thousands of victims died while on these marches.

Deportation Process whereby Nazis removed people from their normal place of residence, often via a deportation centre, to a labour, concentration or death camp.

Der Stürmer Nazi propaganda weekly, luridly antisemitic, founded in 1923 and edited by Julius Streicher.

Displaced persons Those millions of Europeans – Jews and non-Jews – who, by the war's end, had been forced out of their homes, both by Nazi decrees and by the overall effects of the war.

Einsatzgruppen Special mobile units organized by the Reich Security Main Office for the elimination of the Nazis' enemies in countries occupied by them. Primarily responsible for the large-scale massacres of Russian Jews, communists and intellectuals during Operation Barbarossa, 1941, and for the slaughter of Poles throughout the war years.

Final Solution The euphemistic term used by the Nazis for their plans for comprehensive annihilation of European Jewry.

General Government Administrative area in central and southern Poland created by the Nazis following the country's partition between Germany and the Soviet Union. Became the centre of the death camp system.

Genocide A term created by the international jurist Raphael Lemkin in 1943 to denote a conscious attempt at the physical destruction of a defined group of people.

Gestapo The German state secret police. Directly under the control of Himmler from 1936.

Ghetto The quarters of some European towns in which Jews were compulsorily required to reside in the Middle Ages. Resurrected by the Nazis following their take-over of Poland.

Haganah The underground military organization of the Jewish community in Palestine under the British Mandate.

Hitler Youth Organization originally founded in 1926 to inculcate racial, social and militaristic values into young Germans. After 1936, membership for 10–18 year olds.

Judenrat German term meaning 'Jewish Council', used to describe the Jewish representative bodies established by the Nazis in various ghettos and communities. The purpose behind their establishment was to provide the Nazis with vital administrative and supervisory assistance and to implement Nazi decrees.

Labour camp A camp contributing to Germany's wartime production through the use of slave labour, mostly involving prisoners of war, Jews and foreign nationals.

Lebensraum Literally 'living space'. The acquisition of additional *Lebensraum* to be colonized by German people in the east was central to Hitler's racial vision of the future and therefore a key to his foreign policy and military preparations.

Operation Barbarossa The name of the Nazis' military campaign to destroy the Soviet state, starting on 22 June 1941.

Reichstag German parliament, largely ornamental during the Nazi era.

RSHA (*Reichssicherheitshauptamt* – **Reich Security Main Office**) The security apparatus of the Nazi state formed from an amalgamation of the Gestapo and Kripo (criminal) state police forces with the SD (Nazi Party intelligence service) in 1939.

SA (*Sturmabteilung*) Literally 'stormtroopers', also known as Brownshirts. Shock troops of the Nazi Party founded in 1921. Eclipsed by the SS after the 'Night of the Long Knives' of 30 June 1934 when the SA leadership was murdered.

SD (*Sicherheitsdienst*) The security and intelligence wing of the SS founded, under Heydrich, in 1932. The core of the Reich Security Main Office (RHSA) founded in 1939.

SS (*Schutzstaffel*) Literally 'protection squads' also known as Blackshirts. The paramilitary body created in 1925 to protect the Nazi Party and its leader, Hitler. After the Nazi seizure of absolute power, Himmler turned it into the most powerful organization within the state. All functions of the concentration and death camp system were controlled by it.

Vichy France Puppet regime set up in southern France after Nazi conquest. Northern France continued to be ruled directly by Nazi Germany.

Weimar Germany The democratic republican regime that was established in Germany after the First World War. Lasted until Hitler's destruction of democratic government shortly after his accession to power.

Wehrmacht German regular armed forces.

White Paper, 1939 British policy statement of May 1939, rigidly adhered to throughout the war years, restricting the number of Jewish immigrants to Palestine to a total of 75,000 over the subsequent five-year period (i.e. an average of 15,000 per year).

Zionism Jewish nationalist movement that sought a response to antisemitism in the founding of a Jewish national home in Palestine. The outcome would be the creation of the State of Israel in 1948.

Main characters **2**

Mordechai Anielewicz Young Zionist activist who, as head of the Jewish Combat Organization, led (and died in) the Warsaw Ghetto uprising of April–May 1943.

Leo Baeck Leading Jewish rabbi, scholar and spokesman, who became president of the newly formed *Reichsvertretung der deutschen Juden* (National Organization of German Jewry) after the Nazi take-over in 1933. Continued in this role until deported to Theresienstadt.

David Ben-Gurion Zionist leader of the Jewish community in Palestine. Given its slender resources, he was opposed to rescue efforts which might detract from his primary goal of building a Jewish national home in Palestine. In 1961, as Israeli Prime Minister, he used the Eichmann trial as a way of bringing world attention to the facts of the Holocaust.

Walther Darré Nazi head of the Race Office, Agriculture Minister and advocate of the special German relationship between 'blood and soil'. Argued that only pure Aryans could own land and in a series of laws eliminated Jews from all aspects of German agricultural production and trade.

Simon Dubnow Leading Jewish historian whose last words to his fellow-Jews before his deportation in December 1941 from his home in Riga, Latvia, are said to have been 'Write and record!'

Adolf Eichmann Career bureaucrat in the SS who became a specialist in 'Jewish affairs'. He oversaw first the expulsions of Jews from Greater Germany and later the transport and other administrative arrangements necessary for the implementation of the Final Solution. Seized by Israeli agents in Argentina where he had gone into hiding after the war, Eichmann was tried and sentenced to death by an Israeli court in 1961.

Anne Frank German Jewish girl whose poignant diary chronicles two years of hiding in a tiny attic in Amsterdam. Eventually betrayed to the Gestapo in August 1944, she was deported to Auschwitz and died of typhus in Bergen-Belsen in March 1945. Her diary survived the war and has since been translated into over thirty languages. From its pages, her imaginative, inquisitive teenage mind and unshaken belief in a better future transcend the tragic confines of her hiding-place.

Hans Frank Head of the General Government (Nazi-occupied central and southern Poland) – the heartland of the ghetto and death camp system. Exploited its 2.5 million Jewish population for slave labour, while at the same time ensuring their removal through starvation, expulsion and extermination.

Wilhelm Frick Nazi Minister of the Interior until 1943. Responsible for Nazi racial and anti-Jewish legislation, including the 1935 Nuremberg Laws and 1938 'Aryanization' of Jewish businesses.

Bishop Clemens von Galen Catholic Bishop of Münster who publicly criticized the Nazi 'euthanasia' killings in a sermon in August 1941, leading to its official (though not in practice complete) termination. Later imprisoned by the Nazis.

Joseph Goebbels Nazi Minister of Propaganda, organizing in this capacity repeated anti-Jewish campaigns. Responsible for the *Kristallnacht* pogrom in November 1938 and later the deportation of Jews from Berlin. Committed suicide in Hitler's bunker on 30 April 1945.

Hermann Göring Close Nazi associate of Hitler who acquired wide powers over Germany's economy and its war preparations. Responsible for the expropriation of German Jewish assets in the 1930s and the extension of this policy to the whole of Nazi-occupied Europe during the war. Committed suicide at Nuremberg in 1946.

Herschl Grynszpan Seventeen-year-old Jew who assassinated a German official in the Paris embassy in November 1938, in retaliation for the maltreatment and deportation of his parents from Germany to the Polish border. His action precipitated the Kristallnacht pogrom.

Rudolf Hess Hitler's official deputy. Flew to Scotland in a personal attempt to make peace with the British in 1941. Tried for war crimes at Nuremberg and sentenced to life imprisonment.

Reinhard Heydrich Himmler's right-hand man in the SS and head of the SD, the organization's own security police. Jointly responsible with Himmler for the creation of the Nazi police state and concentration camp system. Creator and organizational chief of the *Einsatzgruppen* with executive responsibility for the implementation of the Final Solution. Convened Wannsee Conference in January 1942 for this purpose. From October 1941, he was Reich Protector of the Czech provinces of Bohemia and Moravia which had been incorporated into the Nazi state. Assassinated by Czech agents in cooperation with the British in May 1942.

Heinrich Himmler Head of the SS and Nazi police apparatus, with overall responsibility for eliminating all enemies of Hitler's new order. Also after 1943 Minister of the Interior. Chief architect of the concentration camp system and prime mover and organizer of the Final Solution. Captured by the British in May 1945 and committed suicide.

Paul von Hindenburg Head of the imperial German army in the First World War and last President of the Weimar Republic. His death in 1934 paved the way for the complete consolidation of Nazi power.

Adolf Hitler Austrian-born leader of the Nazi Party, self-styled Führer (absolute leader) of the German people and obsessive Jew-hater. A charismatic demagogue whose mixture of opportunism and planning plunged Europe into the Second World War. His decision, in June 1941, to invade the Soviet Union – the nerve-centre of his mythical 'Jewish–Bolshevik conspiracy' on to which he projected all that he most feared and loathed – precipitated the implementation of the Final Solution. The total defeat of Nazism by the Allies, culminating in the Red

Army's breakthrough to Berlin, led to his suicide in his Chancellery bunker on 30 April 1945.

Rudolf Hoess   Zealous concentration camp functionary who became commandant of Auschwitz and Birkenau. Worked closely with the IG Farben company in the construction of gas chambers and in the use of Zyclon B gas for the extermination of Soviet prisoners of war and later Jews. Hanged by the Polish authorities in 1947.

Chaim Kaplan   Polish Jewish educator and writer whose Warsaw Ghetto diary minutely chronicled its fate until his own deportation to Treblinka in September 1942.

Bernhard Lichtenberg   Courageous Catholic priest who publicly protested at the maltreatment of Jews. Father Lichtenberg was imprisoned for this 'crime' and died in November 1943, while being transferred from Berlin to Dachau concentration camp.

Josef Mengele   Infamous doctor who oversaw 'selections' for the gas chambers in Auschwitz-Birkenau and conducted the most grisly medical experiments on prisoners. After the war, he became one of the most wanted Nazi war criminals, escaping to South America, where he was reported to have died in the mid-1980s.

Heinrich Müller   Head of Gestapo and, as Adolf Eichmann's immediate superior, had responsibility for executing the Final Solution. Relentlessly committed to the bureaucratic murder of millions, this genocidal fanatic evaded capture at the end of the war and disappeared without verifiable trace.

Pastor Martin Niemöller   Heroic German Lutheran priest who publicly criticized the Nazi persecution of the Jews. His outspokenness led to his incarceration in the Sachsenhausen and later Dachau concentration camps. Survived the war and took his message of toleration across the globe.

Marshal Philippe Pétain   Considered saviour of France after its army had collapsed in the First World War. He was acclaimed saviour for the second time in 1940 when, following the French army's defeat, he negotiated a peace treaty with Hitler. The Vichy regime which he led from the south of the country cooperated with the Nazis in the deportation to the death camps of French Jews and Jewish refugees from other parts of Europe.

Pope Pius XII   Head of the Catholic Church during the Second World War. Pursued an equivocal and controversial policy towards Nazism, failing to speak out publicly against its persecution of the Jews. Severely criticized after the war for not doing more to save the Jews (and other civilians) from extermination.

Field Marshal Walter von Reichenau Professional German soldier notorious for his role in wedding the Wehrmacht to the Nazi regime. As chief of the Sixth Army during Operation Barbarossa, he issued an infamous order in October 1941 calling on the Wehrmacht to 'discharge its historical mission of once and for all delivering the German people from the Asiatic-Jewish peril'.

Joachim von Ribbentrop Hitler's Foreign Minister after 1938. Chief architect of the Nazi Non-aggression Pact with Stalin's Soviet Union of August 1939. Hanged at Nuremberg in 1946.

Ernst Röhm Head of the SA Stormtroopers and a potential challenger to Hitler's leadership of the Nazi Party. Murdered in the 'Night of the Long Knives', 1934.

Alfred Rosenberg Baltic German obsessed by the idea that the Russian Revolution was a facet of the 'international Jewish conspiracy'. The Nazis' key exponent of racial theory. As wartime Reich Minister for the Occupied Eastern Territories, Rosenberg concocted schemes for a subjugated Russia, free of Jews and colonized by Germans.

Chaim Rumkowski Controversial and 'despotic' leader of the Jewish Council in the Polish ghetto of Lodz. He believed that by demonstrating their economic indispensability to the Nazis the Jews of Lodz might be spared. He perished in Auschwitz, killed by his fellow-Jews who felt he had betrayed them.

Bernhard Rust Nazi ex-schoolmaster appointed Reich Minister of Science, Education and Culture in 1934. Subordinated school system to the interests of Nazism, which included the 'de-Judaization' of its teachers and pupils.

Oskar Schindler Highly complex member of the Czech Nazi Party; entrepreneur and womanizer, he followed the German army to Cracow, Poland. There he set up a factory near a forced labour camp (Plaszow) where he protected his largely Jewish workforce. Schindler is said to have saved the lives of more then 1,100 Jews, in unique circumstances, during the Holocaust years. (He has since been immortalized in Steven Spielberg's oscar-winning film, *Schindler's List*.)

Albert Speer Hitler's favourite architect and, from 1942 to 1945, Minister for Armaments and War Production. After the war, he alone admitted the guilt of the Nazi regime at the Nuremberg Trial and acknowledged his personal moral responsibility for the use of slave labour in the factories under his control. Condemned for crimes against humanity, he was sentenced to, and served, twenty years in prison.

Franz Stangl Austrian-born policeman involved in the 'euthanasia' programme and later Commandant of Sobibor and Treblinka death camps. Extradited from Brazil in 1967, he was later sentenced by a German court to life imprisonment, dying soon afterwards.

Julius Streicher Nazi publisher of the violently antisemitic weekly *Der Stürmer* and heavily involved in the Jewish boycott and other anti-Jewish campaigns in Hitler's Germany.

Raoul Wallenberg Swedish diplomat in Budapest who, in late 1944, personally intervened, under cover of diplomatic immunity, to save thousands of Hungarian Jews destined for the gas chambers. Disappeared after the Red Army's entry into the city in January 1945.

Chaim Weizmann Zionist leader based in London who attempted, in the summer of 1944, to persuade the British government to bomb the railway lines leading to Auschwitz. Later became first President of the State of Israel.

Robert Weltsch German Zionist whose editorial in the *Jüdische Rundschau*, 'Wear the Yellow Badge with Pride' became a famous riposte to the Nazi anti-Jewish boycott of 1 April 1933.

Christian Wirth German police bureaucrat whose efficient 'euthanasia' killings of the mentally and physically disabled in Germany paved the way for his later promotion within the death camp system, with responsibility for Belzec, Treblinka and Sobibor.

APPENDICES

Appendix A: Hitler and the Jewish Question – extracts from Hitler's writings

Excerpts from '*Mein Kampf*'

Today it is difficult, if not impossible, for me to say when the word 'Jew' first gave me ground for special thoughts. At home I do not remember having heard the word during my father's lifetime. I believe that the old gentleman would have regarded any special emphasis on this term as cultural backwardness. In the course of his life he had arrived at more or less cosmopolitan views which, despite his pronounced national sentiments, not only remained intact, but also affected me to some extent.

Likewise at school I found no occasion which could have led me to change this inherited picture . . .

Not until my fourteenth or fifteenth year did I begin to come across the word 'Jew', with any frequency, partly in connection with political discussions. This filled me with a mild distaste, and I could not rid myself of an unpleasant feeling that always came over me whenever religious quarrels occurred in my presence.

At that time I did not think anything else of the question.

There were few Jews in Linz. In the course of the centuries their outward appearance had become Europeanized and had taken on a human look; in fact, I even took them for Germans. The absurdity of this idea did not dawn on me because I saw no distinguishing feature but the strange religion. The fact that they had, as I believed, been persecuted on this account sometimes almost turned my distaste at unfavourable remarks about them into horror . . . Then I came to Vienna. [Gradually], I encountered the Jewish question . . .

My views with regard to anti-Semitism thus succumbed to the passage of time, and this was my greatest transformation of all.

It cost me the greatest inner soul struggles and only after months of battle between my reason and my sentiments did my reason begin to emerge victorious. Two years later, my sentiment had followed my reason, and from then on became its most loyal guardian and sentinel.

At the time of this bitter struggle between spiritual education and cold reason, the visual instruction of the Vienna streets had performed invaluable services. There came a time when I no longer, as in the first days, wandered blindly through the mighty city; now with open eyes I saw not only the buildings but also the people.

Once, as I was strolling through the Inner City, I suddenly encountered an apparition in a black caftan and black hair locks. Is this a Jew? was my first thought.

For, to be sure, they had not looked like this in Linz. I observed the man furtively and cautiously, but the longer I stared at this foreign face, scrutinizing feature for feature, the more my first question assumed a new form:

Is this a German?

As always in such cases, I now began to try to relieve my doubts by books . . .

I could no longer very well doubt that the objects of my study were not Germans of a special religion, but a people in themselves; for since I had begun to concern myself with this question and to take cognizance of the Jews, Vienna appeared to me in a different light than before. Wherever I went, I began to see Jews, and the more I saw, the more sharply they became distinguished from the rest of humanity . . .

The cleanliness of this people, moral and otherwise, I must say, is a point in itself. By their very exterior you could tell that these were no lovers of water, and, to your distress, you often knew it with your eyes closed. Later I often grew sick to my stomach from the smell of these caftan-wearers. Added to this, there was their unclean dress and generally unheroic appearance.

All this could scarcely be called very attractive; but it became positively repulsive when, in addition to their physical uncleanliness, you discovered the moral stains on this 'chosen people'.

In a short time I was made more thoughtful than ever by my slowly rising insight into the type of activity carried on by the Jews in certain fields.

Was there any form of filth or profligacy, particularly in cultural life, without at least one Jew involved in it?

If you cut even cautiously into such an abscess, you found, like a maggot in a rotting body, often dazzled by the sudden light – a kike [Yid]!

What had to be reckoned heavily against the Jews in my eyes was when I became acquainted with their activity in the press, art, literature and the theatre. All the unctuous reassurances helped little or nothing. It sufficed to look at a bill-board, to study the names of the men behind the horrible trash they advertised, to make you hard for a long time to come. This was pestilence, spiritual pestilence, worse than the Black Death of olden times, and the people was being infected with it! . . .

And now I began to examine my beloved 'world press' from this point of view.

And the deeper I probed, the more the object of my former admiration shrivelled. The style became more and more unbearable; I could not help rejecting the content as inwardly shallow and banal; the objectivity of exposition now seemed to me more akin to lies than honest truth; and the writers were – Jews . . .

The relation of the Jews to prostitution and, even more, to the white-slave traffic, could be studied in Vienna as perhaps in no other city of Western Europe, with the possible exception of the southern French ports. If you walked at night through the streets and alleys of Leopoldstadt, at every step you witnessed proceedings which remained concealed from the majority of the German people until the War gave the soldiers on the eastern front occasion to see similar things, or, better expressed, forced them to see them.

When for the first time I recognized the Jew as the cold-hearted, shameless and calculating director of this revolting vice traffic in the scum of the big city, a cold shudder ran down my back.

But then a flame flared up within me. I no longer avoided discussion of the Jewish question; no, now I sought it. And when I learned to look for the Jew in all branches of cultural and artistic life and its various manifestations, I suddenly encountered him in a place where I would least have expected to find him.

When I recognized the Jew as the leader of the Social Democracy, the scales dropped from my eyes. A long soul struggle had reached its conclusion . . .

Only now did I become thoroughly acquainted with the seducer of our people . . .

The Jewish doctrine of Marxism rejects the aristocratic principle of Nature and replaces the eternal privilege of power and strength by the mass of numbers and their dead weight. Thus it denies the value of personality in man, contests the significance of nationality and race, and thereby withdraws from humanity the premise of its existence and its culture. As a foundation of the universe, this doctrine would bring about the end of any order intellectually conceivable to man. And as, in this greatest of all recognizable organisms, the result of an application of such a law could only be chaos, on earth it could only be destruction for the inhabitants of this planet.

If, with the help of his Marxist creed, the Jew is victorious over the other peoples of the world, his crown will be the funeral wreath of humanity and this planet will, as it did thousands of years ago, move through the ether devoid of men.

Eternal Nature inexorably avenges the infringement of her commands.

Hence today I believe that I am acting in accordance with the will of the Almighty Creator: *by defending myself against the Jew, I am fighting for the work of the Lord* . . .

To what an extent the whole existence of this people is based on a continuous lie is shown incomparably by the *Protocols of the Elders of Zion*, so infinitely hated by the Jews. They are based on a forgery, the Frankfurter Zeitung moans and screams once every week: the best proof that they are authentic . . . For once this book has become the common property of a people, the Jewish menace may be considered as broken . . .

His [i.e. the Jew's] unfailing instinct in such things scents the original soul in everyone, and his hostility is assured to anyone who is not spirit of his spirit. Since the Jew is not the attacked but the attacker, not only anyone who attacks passes as his enemy, but also anyone who resists him. But the means with which he seeks to break such reckless but upright souls is not honest warfare, but lies and slander.

Here he stops at nothing, and in his vileness he becomes so gigantic that no one need be surprised if among our people the personification of the devil as the symbol of all evil assumes the living shape of the Jew.

The ignorance of the broad masses about the inner nature of the Jew, the lack of instinct and narrow-mindedness of our upper classes, make the people an easy victim for this campaign of lies.

While from innate cowardice the upper classes turn away from a man whom the Jew attacks with lies and slander, the broad masses from stupidity or simplicity believe everything. The state authorities either cloak themselves in silence or, what usually happens, in order to put an end to the Jewish press campaign, they persecute the unjustly attacked, which, in the eyes of such an official ass, passes as the preservation of state authority and the safeguarding of law and order.

Slowly fear and the Marxist weapon of Jewry descend like a nightmare on the mind and soul of decent people.

They begin to tremble before the terrible enemy and thus have become his final victim.

The Jew's domination in the state seems so assured that now not only can he call himself a Jew again, but he ruthlessly admits his ultimate national and political designs. A section of his race openly owns itself to be a foreign people, yet even they lie. For while the Zionists try to make the rest of the world believe that the national consciousness of the Jew finds its satisfaction in the creation of a Palestinian state, the Jew again slyly dupes the dumb *Goyim*. It doesn't even enter their heads to build up a Jewish state in Palestine for the purpose of living there; all they want is a central organization for their international world swindle, endowed with its own sovereign rights and removed from the intervention of other states; a haven for convicted criminals and a university for budding crooks.

It is a sign of their rising confidence and sense of security that at a time when one section is still playing the German, Frenchman or Englishman, the other with open effrontery comes out as the Jewish race.

How close they see approaching victory can be seen by the hideous aspect which their relations with the members of other peoples takes on.

With satanic joy in his face, the black-haired Jewish youth lurks in wait for the unsuspecting girl whom he defiles with his blood, thus stealing her from her people. With every means he tries to destroy the racial foundations of the people he has set out to subjugate. Just as he himself systematically ruins women and girls, he does not shrink back from pulling down the blood barriers for others, even on a large scale. It was and it is Jews who bring the negroes into the Rhineland, always with the same secret thought and clear aim of ruining the hated white race by the necessarily resulting bastardization, throwing it down from its cultural and political height, and himself rising to be its master.

For a racially pure people which is conscious of its blood can never be enslaved by the Jew. In this world he will forever be master over bastards and bastards alone.

And so he tries systematically to lower the racial level by a continuous poisoning of individuals.

And in politics he begins to replace the idea of democracy by the dictatorship of the proletariat.

In the organized mass of Marxism he has found the weapon which lets him dispense with democracy and in its stead allows him to subjugate and govern the peoples with a dictatorial and brutal fist.

He works systematically for revolutionization in a two-fold sense: economic and political.

Around peoples who offer too violent a resistance to attack from within he weaves a net of enemies, thanks to his international influence, incites them to war, and finally, if necessary, plants a flag of revolution on the very battlefields.

In economics he undermines the states until the social enterprises which have become unprofitable are taken from the state and subjected to his financial control.

In the political field he refuses the state the means for its self-preservation, destroys the foundations of all national self-maintenance and defense, destroys faith in the leadership, scoffs at its history and past, and drags everything that is truly great into the gutter.

Culturally, he contaminates art, literature, the theatre, makes a mockery of natural feeling, overthrows all concepts of beauty and sublimity, of the noble and the good, and instead drags men down into the sphere of his own base nature.

Religion is ridiculed, ethics and morality represented as outmoded, until the last props of a nation in its struggle for existence in this world have fallen.

Now begins the great last revolution. In gaining political power the Jew casts off the few cloaks that he still wears. The democratic people's Jew becomes the blood-Jew and tyrant over peoples. In a few years he tries to exterminate the national intelligentsia and by robbing the peoples of their natural intellectual leadership makes them ripe for the slave's lot of permanent subjugation.

The most frightful example of this kind is offered by Russia, where he killed or starved about thirty million people with positively fanatical savagery, in part amid inhuman tortures, in order to give a gang of Jewish journalists and stock exchange bandits domination over a great people.

The end is not only the end of the freedom of the peoples oppressed by the Jew, but also the end of this parasite upon the nations. After the death of his victim, the vampire sooner or later dies too.

Source: Adolf Hitler, Mein Kampf *('My Struggle'), Munich, 1925 (Houghton Mifflin, Boston, 1943; Hutchinson, London, 1969) quoted in Paul Mendes-Flohr and Jehuda Reinharz,* The Jew in the Modern World *(Oxford University Press, 1980) and in Yitzhak Arad, Yisrael Gutman and Abraham Margaliot (eds),* Documents on the Holocaust *(Yad Vashem Publications, 1981)*

Extracts from *Hitler's Secret Book* (*c.* 1928)

Just as every people...possesses a powerful urge for self-preservation as its driving force, likewise is it exactly so with Jewry, too. Only here, in accord with their basically different dispositions, the struggle for existence of Aryan peoples and Jewry is also different in its forms. The foundation of the Aryan struggle for life is the soil, which he cultivates and which provides the general basis for an economy satisfying primarily its own needs within its own orbit through the productive forces of its own people.

Because of the lack of productive capacities of its own the Jewish people cannot carry out the construction of a state, viewed in a territorial sense, but as a support of its own existence it needs the work and creative activities of other nations. Thus the existence of the Jew himself becomes a parasitical one within the lives of other peoples. Hence the ultimate goal of the Jewish struggle for existence is the enslavement of productively active peoples. In order to achieve this goal, which in reality has represented Jewry's struggle for existence at all times, the Jew makes use of all weapons that are in keeping with the whole complex of his character.

Therefore in domestic politics within the individual nations he fights first for equal rights and later for super-rights. The characteristics of cunning, intelligence, astuteness, knavery, dissimulation, etc., rooted in the character of his folkdom, serve him as weapons thereto. They are as much strategems in his war of survival as those of other peoples in combat.

In foreign policy he tries to bring other nations into a state of unrest, to divert them from their true interests, and to plunge them into reciprocal wars and in this way gradually rise to mastery over them with the help of the power of money and propaganda.

His ultimate goal is the denationalization, the promiscuous bastardization of other peoples, the lowering of the racial level of the highest peoples as well as the domination of this racial mish-mash through the extirpation of the folkish intelligentsia and its replacement by the members of his own people.

The end of the Jewish world struggle therefore will always be a bloody Bolshevization. In truth this means the destruction of all the intellectual upper classes linked to their peoples so that he can rise to become master of a mankind become leaderless...

The economic conquest of Europe by the Jews was pretty much completed around the turn of the century, and now he began to safeguard it politically. That means, the first attempts to extirpate the national intelligentsia were undertaken in the form of revolutions.

He utilized the tensions between European nations, which are in great part to be ascribed to their general need for territory with the consequences which arise therefrom, for his own advantage by systematically inciting them to the World War.

The aim is the destruction of inherently anti-Semitic Russia as well as the destruction of the German Reich which in the administration and the army still offers resistance to the Jew. The further aim is the overthrow of those dynasties which had not yet been made subject to a democracy dependent upon and led by Jews . . .

The bitterest struggle for the victory of Jewry at the present time is being waged in Germany. Here it is the National Socialist movement which alone has taken upon itself the struggle against this execrable crime against mankind . . .

Source: Hitlers Zweites Buch *(Stuttgart, 1928); English translation:* Hitler's Secret Book *(New York, 1961)*

Appendix B: Reichstag Election Results, 1919–33

Political party	Date of election									
	19 Jan. 1919	6 June 1920	4 May 1924	7 Dec. 1924	20 May 1928	14 Sept. 1930	31 July 1932	6 Nov. 1932	5 Mar. 1933	12 Nov. 1933
1 Nazis	—	—	32 (6.5)	14 (3)	12 (2.6)	107 (18.3)	230 (37.3)	196 (33.1)	288 (43.9)	661 (92.1)
2 Nationalists	44 (10.3)*	71 (13.9)	95 (19.5)	103 (20.5)	73 (14.2)	41 (7.0)	37 (5.9)	52 (8.8)	52 (8.0)	—
3 Small and splinter parties	5 (0.9)	9 (0.8)	29 (6.0)	29 (6.0)	51 (10.0)	72 (12.0)	11 (2.2)	12 (2.2)	7 (2.0)	—
4 People's Party	19 (4.4)	65 (13.9)	45 (9.2)	51 (10.1)	45 (8.7)	30 (4.5)	7 (1.2)	11 (1.9)	2 (0.5)	—
5 Bavarian People's Party	—	21	16	19	16	19	22	20	18	—
6 Centre	91 (19.7)	64 (13.6)	65 (13.4)	69 (13.6)	62 (12.1)	68 (11.8)	75 (12.4)	70 (11.9)	74 (11)	—
7 Democrats	75 (18.6)	39 (8.3)	28 (5.7)	32 (6.3)	25 (4.9)	20 (3.8)	4 (1.0)	2 (1.0)	5 (0.9)	—
8 Social Democrats	165 (37.9)	102 (21.6)	100 (20.5)	131 (26)	153 (29.8)	143 (24.5)	133 (21.6)	121 (20.4)	120 (18.2)	—
9 Independent Social Democrats**	22 (7.6)	84 (17.9)	— (0.8)	— (0.3)	— (0.1)	—	—	—	—	—
10 Communists	—	4 (2.1)	62 (12.6)	45 (9.0)	54 (10.6)	77 (13.1)	89 (14.3)	100 (16.9)	81 (12.2)	—
Total number of seats in Reichstag	421	459	472	493	491	577	608	584	647	661
Total turnout (%)	83	79.2	77.4	78.8	75.6	81.9	84.0	80.6	88.5	95.3

Notes: * Figure in brackets = percentage of votes cast (no data available for Bavarian's People's Party).

** The Independent Social Democratic Party ceased to exist after 1924. Some of its members went back to the Social Democrats and the rest joined the Communists.

Source: Yitzhak Arad, Yisrael Gutman and Abraham Margaliot (eds), *Documents on the Holocaust* (Yad Vashem Publications, 1981), Document 6

Appendix C:
The Second World War at a glance

On 1 September 1939 the Germans launched an invasion of Poland. Two days later the Second World War started when, much to Hitler's surprise, Britain and France, remaining faithful to their undertaking to Poland, declared war on Germany. Nevertheless, within three weeks Germany had completely crushed Poland in a *Blitzkrieg* – a lightning military campaign coordinated between air and ground forces.

Most significantly, one week before the assault on Poland, Hitler had negotiated a secret non-aggression treaty with Stalin (the Molotov-Ribbentropp Pact, so named after the respective Foreign Ministers of the Soviet Union and Nazi Germany). For the fourth time in its history Poland was divided between Russia and Germany. The western and northern districts were annexed to the Greater German Reich, the eastern provinces ceded to the Soviet Union, as previously agreed in the Molotov-Ribbentropp Pact. The central section around Lublin, Cracow and the Polish capital Warsaw became a German colony, known as the General Government.

After several months of military inactivity, the German armies conquered and occupied one country after another in rapid succession: Denmark and Norway (April 1940), Holland and Belgium (May 1940) and France (June 1940). Defeated France was split into two regions: the larger, northern territory was ruled directly by Germany; the southern sector was unoccupied and known as Vichy France. Germany's inability to overcome stout British resistance, despite massive and intimidating aerial bombardment, led Hitler to turn his attention to the east and to prepare for the invasion of the Soviet Union. This had always been his principal ideological objective, as he makes clear in *Mein Kampf*.

In the spring of 1941 the German army under General Rommel captured much of North Africa, while in the Balkans it overran both Greece and Yugoslavia. Everywhere the German army was triumphant and seemingly invincible. The countries of south-eastern Europe – Bulgaria, Romania and Hungary – became German satellites, while Italy was, at first, Germany's principal European ally.

With Britain alone holding out, Hitler then made a blunder that was to prove fatal to his ambitions for sustained European domination. On 22 June 1941, he tore up his treaty with Stalin and attacked the Soviet Union with all his might. By October his forces had reached the gates of Moscow and Leningrad and, by the end of 1941, had taken extensive areas of Russia's western empire, including most of the Ukraine. The freezing Russian winter, however, severely hampered the progress of his offensive.

On 7 December 1941, Germany's eastern ally Japan mounted a surprise – and, as it turned out, extremely rash – attack on the American naval base at Pearl Harbour in Hawaii. Thus the USA, with her enormous military and industrial capacity, entered the conflict, with both Germany and Italy declaring war on her on 11 December 1941.

Two turning points in the conflict occurred in 1942/3, which heralded the start of a fundamental change in the course of the war to the advantage of the anti-Nazi Allies. In the North African desert the British under the command of General Montgomery seriously weakened Rommel's legendary German army in winning the battle of El-Alamein. Similarly, in January 1943, in a victory that was just as psychologically crucial, Soviet troops counter-attacked and won a decisive victory at Stalingrad over seemingly indestructible German forces.

By the end of November 1943, the Allies had taken possession of southern Italy. In 1944, while the Russians were advancing westwards into Poland and Romania, British and American troops landed on the beaches of Normandy (6 June – D-Day) and began the liberation of France and Belgium.

With Allied armies advancing into Germany on two fronts, the frenzied defence of Berlin became the backdrop for the eventual suicide of Adolf Hitler at the end of April 1945. Germany surrendered on 7 May. The war in the Pacific, however, continued, and only after the Soviet entry into the Pacific War and the dropping of two atomic bombs on Hiroshima and Nagasaki did the Japanese capitulate. They would surrender unconditionally on 14 August 1945. The war was now over.

Appendix D: Nazi Europe, 1939–45: Statistics of Jewish dead

Numbers of Jews Murdered in Europe: An Estimate

Country	Jewish population September 1939	Number of Jews murdered	Percentage of Jews murdered
1 Poland	3,300,000	2,800,000	85.0
2 USSR (occupied territories)	2,100,000	1,500,000	71.4
3 Romania	850,000	425,000	50.0
4 Hungary	404,000	200,000	49.5
5 Czechoslovakia	315,000	260,000	82.5
6 France	300,000	90,000	30.0
7 Germany	210,000	170,000	81.0
8 Lithuania	150,000	135,000	90.0
9 Holland	150,000	90,000	60.0
10 Latvia	95,000	85,000	89.5
11 Belgium	90,000	40,000	44.4
12 Greece	75,000	60,000	80.0
13 Yugoslavia	75,000	55,000	73.3
14 Austria	60,000	40,000	66.6
15 Italy	57,000	15,000	26.3
16 Bulgaria	50,000	7,000	14.0
17 Others	20,000	6,000	30.0
Total	8,301,000	5,978,000	72.0

Source: Leon Poliakov and Josef Wulf (eds), Das Dritte Reich und die Juden: Dokumente und Aufsätze *(Arani-Verlag, GmbH, 1955), cited in Paul Mendes-Flohr and Jehuda Reinharz,* The Jew in the Modern World *(Oxford University Press, 1980)*

Appendix E: Teaching the Holocaust: Dilemmas and considerations

There are many methodological traps into which teachers of the Holocaust can fall. They should try to find a balance, or steer a course, between the following extremes (Scylla and Charybdis).

('It is the nature of dilemmas that whenever one takes one side or another and stretches it to its utmost limits, one is in danger of bringing one's case *ad absurdum*. This is perhaps the tragic dimension of the term "dilemma": one cannot choose between two or more possibilities but has to consider them, knowing the limits and shortcomings of each of them. Guided by educational rather than by ideological deliberation, this consideration should be done, not by taking this side or another, but by reflecting on all possibilities and by considering their implications.' [Chaim Schatzker])

SCYLLA	*CHARYBDIS*
Overall approach	
1 **Insistence on uniqueness**	**Surrender to banality**
(a) An approach which stresses the incomparable abnormality of the Holocaust (Nazism demonized).	The Holocaust as a mere symbol for the baseness of human nature.
(b) 'Planet Auschwitz'.	Holocaust susceptible to clinical, academic analysis, translatable into modern educational forms, e.g. simulation (ugh!).
(c) An approach that deals only with the particular lessons for Jews (Holocaust deuniversalized).	Holocaust located (lost?) in host of disciplines, eg. moral education, psychology, theology, general history (Holocaust deJudaized).
2 **Perspective** Approach that is strictly chronological and 'historical'.	Approach that deals only with the ethical, psychological and/or theological dimensions.
3 **Tone** 'Emotional' approach	An approach that is too dispassionate and 'academic'.

Dilemmas within subject

1   Theories on the nature of antisemitism and Nazi ideology

(a) Antisemitism unique, 'cosmic' and timeless.

Antisemitism one (extreme) form of 'prejudice'.

(b) Holocaust 'logical' product of 2,000 year continuum.

Nazism essentially a parable for the darker side of modernity. Therefore Holocaust may be torn from context of Jewish history and history of anti-semitism.

(c) Antisemitism *central* to Nazi ideology *and* policy.

Nazi antisemitism purely instrumental ('scapegoat' theory).

(d) Jews as *special* victims of Nazism.

Jews, Slavs, Gypsies, homosexuals, etc. as equal victims.

(e) Final Solution planned over long term.

Final Solution essentially improvised.

(f) Killing Jews more important than winning war.

Holocaust as by-product of Second World War.

2   The theological 'meaning' of the Holocaust

(a) Holocaust can be explained *with* God.

Holocaust can be explained only without God.

(b) Fackenheim's '614th Commandment' – interpretation (i).

Fackenheim's '614th Commandment' – interpretation (ii).

(c) Holocaust 'proves' bankruptcy of 'Christian' civilization.

Holocaust essentially an attack on Christianity itself.

3   The bystanders

'All are responsible'.

'None are responsible'.

4   Significance of Hitler

'One madman is to blame'.

'It could have happened without Hitler'.

5   Jewish behaviour

Emphasis on Jewish passivity and virtual 'collaboration' in their own destruction.

Exaggerating the incidence of Jewish resistance, physical and spiritual (overcompensation).

6   The Holocaust and Israel

(a) Israel as a Jewish answer to Hitler.

Israel as essentially a product of nineteenth-century Jewish/European history

(b) Post-Holocaust 'Jewish survival' as an end in itself.

The *content* of Jewish/Israeli survival as decisive.

Note

This chart was produced by the author to accompany and illustrate a series of lectures given to teachers and trainee teachers, drawn from many different humanities disciplines, during the mid-1980s. It was written in a kind of shorthand and was not meant to be free-standing and self-explanatory. For example, 'Fackenheim's 614th Commandment', alluded to in 2(b) under the heading 'theological "meaning" of the Holocaust', is that additional Jewish 'commandment' postulated by the philosopher and theologian Emil Fackenheim in *The Jewish Return to History* (Schocken Books, 1978), which may be paraphrased as 'Thou shalt not hand Hitler a posthumous victory'. Like many Jewish commandments, this has proved susceptible to several quite different and, in this particular instance, opposing interpretations.

The chart is included here to show one way of presenting some of the conceptual, historiographical and methodological difficulties and dilemmas involved in teaching the Holocaust. It also represents, to a degree, some of the early thinking on which this book – and other works by the author – would eventually be built.

Appendix F: The nature and development of human prejudice

PREJUDICE (adverse)

Stereotype (Generalized notion)

Discrimination, Alienation, Harassment: social, legal, psychological and physical

Motivation

Ignorance, fear, suspicion, anger, doubt, inability to define (fear of unknown), frustration (e.g. *economic* sexual, political), deeds or misdeeds, real and imagined, of individual, associated with whole group, culturally transmitted ('inherited') antagonism

NB *projection* and *displacement*

Outright assault: legal and/or physical

Exclusion, removal, 'Elimination'?

Area of 'Difference'

Religion, race, nationality, culture, lifestyle, age, sexuality, gender, class, social background, accent, economic position, level of education, in-group v. out-group, majority v. minority, minority v. majority, *any* perceivable *difference* (e.g. height, left handedness, etc.)

NB *power* v. *powerlessness*

Possible 'Victim' Responses

1 'Alienation'
   (a) Rejection of self and own group – 'self and own group hatred' – seeing oneself and one's own group through the eyes of others. 'Surrender' to dominant host culture and denial of own group culture
   (b) Rejection of society outside group – over-reliance on own group, introspection
2 Over-sensitivity – seeing 'prejudice' both where it exists and where it does not exist
3 Self-assertiveness as a weapon to 'fight back' – aggression, ambition, 'over-achievement'
4 'Counter-prejudice', sometimes translated into action, e.g. anti-social behaviour, certain kinds of rebellion or even 'terrorism'

Appendix G: Intentionalists v. Functionalists: The debate among historians

Note: This appendix is intended primarily for teachers and Advanced Level history specialists.

During the 1980s and early 1990s there was a major historiographical divide among Holocaust historians – especially in Germany – with protagonists being polarized into broadly two camps. On the one hand, there were the so-called 'intentionalists', who – briefly stated – argued that the mass annihilation of the Jews was always intended and that it was essentially a question of when, rather than whether, Hitler would implement his consistently held fantasies about a Jew-free Europe (or even world). To the 'intentionalists', the part played by Hitler was not only inspirational but, in terms of planning and implementation, utterly central. The most prominent historians in the 'intentionalist' camp are Lucy Dawidowicz, Gerald Fleming, Eberhard Jäckel and Karl Hildebrand.

In the other camp were to be found the so-called 'functionalist' or 'structuralist' school of historians, who broadly argued that the Holocaust was not so much the consequence of long-term, coherent planning – ordered, as it were, from the top of the Nazi state down – as blundered into, as a bureaucratic and decidedly *ad hoc* solution to their perceived 'Jewish problem', especially once the invasion of the Soviet Union was being planned and indeed undertaken. Views about the critical importance of the part played by Adolf Hitler varied considerably among the 'functionalists'. Some believed that the Final Solution was not so much willed and decreed by Hitler as improvised by the bureaucrats; competing for favour in Hitler's eyes, they devised a solution to their leader's 'Jewish problem' as a means of shoring up their own position within the corridors of power. The Final Solution was thus seen as a major triumph for bureaucrats like Himmler and eventually Eichmann. The 'functionalist' historians include Martin Broszat, Christopher Browning and Hans Mommsen.

One of the more engaging and moderately iconoclastic 'functionalists' is the American historian Arno Mayer, who caused hackles to rise throughout the American-Jewish academic and 'political' establishment with his challenging – though, in the final analysis, resistible and unproven – view that the Final Solution was in essence an act of 'sour grapes', embarked upon only once the German campaign in the Soviet Union had started to go badly wrong, rather than the apogee of Hitler's triumphalism. In this view, the early phase of mass shootings by the *Einsatzgruppen* would have to be seen as a quite separate programmatic (and even ideological) phase from the post-Wannsee Conference industrialized Final Solution stage (i.e. the death camps).

Generally speaking, 'intentionalists' tend to the view that the Holocaust is an incomparably unique historical phenomenon, while the 'functionalists' are, perhaps predictably, more likely to adopt a more universal, relativist stance. Interestingly, Daniel Jonah Goldhagen, whose controversial, block-busting work *Hitler's Willing Executioners* came close to indicting the entire German people for their acceptance of 'eliminationist antisemitism', claims that his work lies outside the 'intentionalist'/'functionalist' debate. Others, though, might readily place him to the extreme right of the 'intentionalist' camp.

In my earlier work *The Nazi Holocaust* I tried to steer a middle course between these and other polar positions – for instance the dichotomy of uniqueness versus universality – recognizing where there were elements of each position that merited serious consideration (see also Appendix E, p. 172). For example, I argued that while Hitler's pure, full-blooded anti-Jewish *ideology* – the fantasy, if you like, of a Jew-free Europe – may be interpreted from relatively early days as aiming at an extermination, the Nazi government's anti-Jewish *policy* quite clearly did not. The policy right up to 1939, and in western and central Europe probably beyond 1939, was aimed at creating the intolerable conditions necessary to induce a 'voluntary' migration, even among those Jews fiercely proud of their German, Austrian and Czech identities; it was only the palpable refusal by other countries to relax their harsh immigration restrictions and the eventual exhaustion or inappropriateness – as the Nazis saw it – of other alternatives (e.g. the plan for the mass evacuation of Jews to Madagascar) that would lead to a definite shift in policy, away from forced migration to one of ghettoization and eventual annihilation.

Index